My Ever Dear Charlie

My Ever Dear Charlie

Letters Home from the Dakota Territory

EDITED BY ARTHUR GIBBS DRAPER

*with the assistance of Doris King Draper
and Carolyn Draper Joslyn Doyle*

TWODOT®

GUILFORD, CONNECTICUT
HELENA, MONTANA

AN IMPRINT OF THE GLOBE PEQUOT PRESS

A · T W O D O T® · B O O K

Copyright © 2006 by The Draper Family Trust

TwoDot is a registered trademark of Morris Book Publishing, LLC.

Text design: Lisa Reneson
All illustrations and photographs courtesy The Draper Family unless otherwise noted.

Library of Congress Cataloging-in-Publication Data
My ever dear Charlie: letters home from the Dakota Territory / the Draper Family Trust.
    —1st ed.
        p. cm.
    Letters written by members of the Draper family, chiefly Fannie McClurg Draper, from the Dakota Territory.
    Includes bibliographical references.
    ISBN 0-7627-3952-5
    1. Draper, Fannie McClurg, 19th cent.—Correspondence. 2. Women pioneers—South Dakota—Correspondence. 3. Pioneers—South Dakota—Correspondence. 4. Draper family—Correspondence. 5. Frontier and pioneer life—South Dakota. 6. South Dakota—Social life and customs—19th century. 7. South Dakota—Biography. 8. Walworth County (S.D.)—Biography. I. Draper, Fannie McClurg, 19th cent. II. Draper Family Trust.
F655.M9 2005
978.3'1802'0922—dc22

                                                                          2005017699

Manufactured in the United States of America
First Edition/First Printing

CONTENTS

ACKNOWLEDGMENTS

WE ARE GRATEFUL TO A GOOD NUMBER of people who have taken an interest in these letters. Irene Bennett Brown provided the single-most crucial boost when she saw the letters' importance and stirred up some curiosity in her network of writers and historians. We are very grateful to Irene, and to Erin Turner of The Globe Pequot Press, for seeing a need to tell this, as Fannie put it, "tip top story." Lynne Morrow, director of the Local Records Program in the Missouri Secretary of State's Office, has been a friend of the Draper-McClurg Family Papers, responsible for getting the papers archived and available to the public, with cooperation from our cousin, the late Emma Gibbs Draper Phillips. We acknowledge the service of the Western Historical Manuscript Collection at the University of Missouri in Columbia for its stewardship of the Draper-McClurg Family Papers (C3069). Audrey and Dennis Beitelspacher, the present owners of the land where the Drapers lived over the winter of 1886–87, have been wonderful to work with, letting us prowl over the ground on several occasions, answering our questions, and providing pictures of the place under snow. Thanks also to the Wilding Studios of Hermann, Missouri, for their work preparing drawings and diorama for publication. The two best writers in the Draper family since Fannie McClurg Draper are Anne Draper Worland and Jill Draper Cook, and both offered some very helpful suggestions for getting this all put together. Finally, Dorie Draper and Carolyn Doyle, besides creating the art work and the diorama, have traveled every step of the way in this publication venture, and it would not have happened without them.

Fannie McClurg Draper as a young woman.

INTRODUCTION

THE LETTERS OF FANNIE AND CHARLIE DRAPER'S family to and from the Dakota Territory of the late 1880s, are uniquely intimate and present vivid insights into frontier life. Their distinction derives from the purpose in writing them—to keep the family together, to assure that the father, back in Missouri, was abreast of all the daily issues, developments, and stresses his family was undergoing on the Dakota frontier. Fannie's letters vividly portray the mundane matters of cooking, doing the wash, and cleaning in a remote Dakota soddy. Fannie McClurg Draper's kindly charm, loving disposition, and gracious gentleness blend with an honest, earthy, witty, forceful, practical, determined strength of character to make her a compelling narrator for the Draper Dakota story. The other voices represented here are interesting and authentic, too, and add rich context to the narrative, but Fannie's voice is the one you remember.

Her letters tell of her providing for the education and welfare of her big family, in cramped quarters, with her patrician father and put-upon brother always looking on. The letters tell of the family's enduring the famous blizzard of 1886-87 and of Fannie's suffering a disfiguring attack of erysipelas. Through all this stress, we see Fannie diligently keeping an eye on the business of the doomed homesteading enterprise, while keeping family traditions, morale, and identity alive. And there is always the over-arching challenge of negotiating within the complex and sometimes conflicting roles of dutiful wife, rational woman, and responsible mother.

Snowbound in a sod shanty on the plains of the Dakota territory in one of the worst winters in memory, with six children (aged thirteen to one year and still nursing), an elderly patriarch, a mildly disgruntled bachelor brother, and a tribe of in-laws who popped in to freeload from time to time—this woman, who just twenty years before hosted "at homes" in Washington, D.C., for her congressman father—kept this flawed venture on track with grace, love, hard work, and reasonably good humor, for a full year. And she writes with a skill that evokes the sights, sounds, smells, textures, and emotion of this powerful experience on the Dakota plains.

The decision to homestead in Dakota came within a chain of circumstances in McClurg-Draper-Johnson family fortunes, and was a bold and ambitious gesture toward starting a large-scale ranching and farming enterprise in the West.[1] In 1885 Draper's brother-in-law, Marshall Johnson, and two of his sons had filed claims in the Dakota Territory and had a very profitable year. The weather their first winter in Dakota was moderate, the moisture was ample, and cattle thrived on the prairie grasses. Their very positive experience in what is now central South Dakota ignited flames of ambition and adventure in the McClurg-Draper-Johnson clan, and a plan developed for a general migration of the families to Dakota Territory. The move was ambitious—to set up a cooperative family enterprise to establish a foothold for an expanding farming and ranching enterprise in the west.

The fact that it was a discretionary, entrepreneurial venture explains, in some measure, Fannie's freedom to entertain disillusionment. On the one hand, Fannie feels required to be a dutiful, traditional wife, to defer to her husband's wisdom. The mainspring in Fannie's moti-

---

1 Appendix B contains a short summary of the Draper-McClurg political and economic involvements before and just after the Civil War in Missouri.

*Veterans of the Dakota trip (and other family members) gathered in 1904. From the left, back row: **Jim Draper, Uncle Joe McClurg, Emma, Joe,** Clint Draper (Mame's husband), **Mame,** Annie Laurie Draper (Arthur's wife), **Arthur, Charlie** (holding Arthur and Annie's daughter Polly's hand), and **Kate** (seated). **Fannie** is seated in front, holding Arthur and Annie's son Ned. Governor McClurg had died four years before this picture was taken.*

vation had been the Biblical "Whither thou goest I will go." But the "thou" in her situation had stayed home! Fannie's husband Charles, whose name was on the homesteading agreements stipulating his residence on the homestead, was there only briefly during the term of the "proving up." On the other hand, Fannie is a bright, worldly, and competent woman and responsible mother in intimate contact with the stark realities before her. The two viewpoints are sometimes irreconcilable, but she has only a limited set of tools for influencing events. And, hovering in the background is the message from home that her brother Jim, secure with his dental practice back in Missouri, had suggested that she was perhaps lacking in grit! Poor Fannie. Grit, indeed.

There is no need for Fannie to apologize to her brother Jim or any-one else for her grit quotient. A lot more people left Dakota than stayed there, after the Dakota boom went bust. In the late 1880s, according to the plat of Walworth County, in township 121 N., Range 75 W. (where the Drapers' property was located), there were 165 landowners, with nearly all owning 160 or more acres. Toward the end of the twentieth century, the plat for the same township shows only fifty-five landowners, with a small handful owning several sections (thus earning their living from the land) and most with eighty acres or less and likely not depend-ent exclusively on farming for a livelihood. None of the surnames that appeared on the nineteenth century township plat also appear on the twentieth century plat.

Put another way, over the years, for every settler resembling Willa Cather's Alexandra Bergson, there were many more resembling Fannie Draper. And grit, as Fannie declares, had nothing to do with it. What seemed at one point a plausible alternative for a satisfactory life turned out, after some actual experience, not to be plausible after all. Most peo-ple—especially if there were an attractive option, as there was in Fannie's case—would likely have felt as she did about the Dakota decision.

The party that left Lebanon, Missouri, in June of 1886 included the sixty-eight year old patriarch, J.W. McClurg, former Republican U.S. congressman and governor of Missouri; his forty-year-old daughter, Frances (Fannie); Fannie's children Arthur (thirteen), Mame (twelve), Jim (ten), Joe (seven), Kate (four), and Emma (just turned one and nurs-ing); Fannie's brother Joe (thirty-eight); and a hired man, Mr. Lattimore, who drove and helped with the work in exchange for the opportunity to go to Dakota.

Shortly after they arrived in Walworth County, after about a month of travel with mules (Alie and Pete) and a wagon, Charles joined them to get them settled in and the farming operation under way. He stayed several weeks, then returned by train to Lebanon, where he continued to hold his job in the bank to supply cash to support the venture. He was bound to his job in Lebanon for the duration of the experience.

The family's original intention was to take ownership of the quarter section in Walworth County under provisions of the 1862 Homestead Act, which required five years living on and working the land, along with making required improvements. One of the themes in the letters is stress about Charles's meeting the homesteading requirements, and nothing in the letters really nails down what happened, although it is clear that Charles did eventually get full ownership of the land. Charlie had three years of credit as a Union Civil War veteran to apply to the five-year residence requirement. The letters suggest that a Mr. Terro (a neighbor) had built the house and well that were on the property when Fannie arrived, so the required improvements had been made before the Drapers took possession. Charlie counted on his family's residence to count toward the five-year requirement. The fact that his wife and family had met the letter and spirit of the law counted for nothing. At one point, Fannie indignantly inquires, "What does a poor woman amount to? I wonder why a man should ever condescend to marry one."

When it became clear that the family's staying in Dakota was not going to work out, the fall-back position was a provision in the law that, at any time, the applicant could pay the government $1.25 per acre, and, with six months' residency, get title to the land. Charlie clearly hoped his time spent on the homestead, added to the fact that his family lived there uninterruptedly for a full year, could be interpreted to meet the requirement: It was not uncommon for the head of the household to go find work to support his family on the homestead, after the growing season was over. Legal advice about the technicalities was, at best, ambiguous.[2]

The Walworth County real estate records contain a "receiver's receipt" reflecting that CC Draper bought the property for $200 in November, 1890, about three years after the family left. In 1892 a warranty deed in the Recorder's Office proves that he sold his 160 acres to Nellie T. Maines for $2000. That seems a reasonable profit, but, ironically, the same deal might have been made without Fannie and the children ever leaving Missouri in June of 1886. The horrendous year they spent fighting mosquitoes in summer and blizzards in winter in the Dakota sod house actually accounted for nothing.[3]

Nothing, that is, except this remarkable set of letters recording the experience of that remarkable year. Many others suffered through that winter, of course, and there are many other vivid records of that terrible time. Because the railroads were aggressively recruiting settlers and because there had been several years of moderate and moist weather in the north central plains, the Dakota boom was cresting.

Cattlemen, on a much larger scale than the Johnsons, had imported thousands of head of cattle to the area. Many of them were driven up from relatively moderate climates, such as Texas, and thus were not accli-

---

2 Letters refer to a "trial" at Aberdeen involving a tree claim. The only patent ever issued Charles Draper was for a "Sale—Cash Entry," not a tree claim. See Appendix A in which Charles provides notes giving some details about the property transactions.

3 We know that Fannie's brother Joe stayed in Dakota for some time after his sister and the children left, and Governor McClurg stayed more than a year longer, and there is no record of his or the Governor's proving up on their own homesteads, though there is mention of their working on them. Although a letter indicates that the Governor is working and rooming at a store in Bowdle in the fall of 1888, it is not clear whether he or his son Joe may have stayed on the Draper homestead for part of the time, at least, after the Drapers left. Nothing in the family papers clears this up, though there is some documentation that Joe McClurg was still farming in Dakota in 1894. The Governor received an appointment from the Harrison administration to administer the Federal Land Office in Springfield, Missouri, in 1889; his Dakota experience gave him more qualifications for the job than the typical patronage appointee.

mated to harsh winter conditions. The winter of 1886–87 was disastrous—the worst in many years—with snows beginning in November and continuing through March and sustained periods of -40 degree temperatures. Cattlemen had felt no need to make provisions for shelter for the animals. West of Walworth County, the "Turkey-Track" and "E6" cattle companies, who had shipped in 27,000 head of cattle the summer of 1886, were able to round up only 250 of them—more than a 99-percent loss—by the next summer. Cattle drifted south in search of shelter and gathered in ravines to get out of the wind and were caught there by the deep snows. In the spring, "skeletons of steers littered the rangeland. Bones . . . were massed in gulches and valleys. Nature thoughtfully sent flash floods to wash these odorous remains of one-time herds down the rivers."[4]

Another vivid account in the Bismarck, Dakota, newspaper described conditions on February 11, 1887:

There is serious apprehension that there will be an appalling loss of human lives in Montana and western Dakota. Snow began falling early in November and there is more on the ground than for ten years. Most of the stage roads are entirely closed up and trains are running at irregular intervals, some being four or five days apart and the supply of fuel is becoming almost exhausted. The snow is drifted to enormous depths and should another protracted storm occur it is believed that hundreds would succumb to its terrors. As it is more people have frozen to death this winter than for a quarter of a century. The cold has been intense. Reports are coming in from the Dakota ranges of the large losses of cattle owing to the scarcity of feed and insufficient protection. . . . Many cattlemen left their ranch

---

4 "An Autobiography of a Cowman," *South Dakota Historical Collections*, Vol. XI, p. 512.

houses during a storm and never returned, and women and children lost their way between the stable and house freezing to death often-times within a few yards of their own doorsteps.[5]

With plenty of coal and provisions laid by and a snug sod house, the Drapers had only the mules, claustrophobia, and homesickness to worry about. They were fortunate to have lost no lives nor significant fortune that winter. The Johnson in-laws, however, lost a number of cat-tle of their own and had contracted with other homesteaders to herd their cattle. The letters vividly describe their painful searches for cattle in blizzards. Fannie's descriptions of her brother Joe's struggles with the snow around the homestead leave a powerful impression. Even today, with immense four-wheel drive tractors, heated cabs, and cell phones, Dennis and Audrey Beitelspacher, who now own the property the Drapers homesteaded, get "the thousand-mile stare" in their eyes when they talk of being out in a South Dakota blizzard.

In her letter of February 9, 1887, Fannie fantasizes whimsically about someone needing to write up their Dakota story in the future, suggesting that she "give the points and some ideas" and Charlie "do the filling," and together they can "make a tiptop story." Fannie's fine eye for detail, her good ear for the telling phrase, and her gracious and kindly personality emerge clearly in these letters. She writes with remarkable skill, wit, and insight, and the result is a powerful record of the daily life of a strong nineteenth century American family under sig-nificant stress.

We are gratified that, with publishing these letters now 119 years later, we are finally helping Fannie tell her "tiptop story." And we do not

---

5 "Ranching and Stock Raising in Dakota," *South Dakota Historical Collections,* Vol. XIV, pp. 457–58.

feel any regret at the role reversal—with Fannie telling the story and Charlie and others supplying occasional "points" and "ideas."[6]

Notes on Editing the Letters

Transcribing and editing the letters has been relatively simple. Most of the correspondents had wonderful penmanship, so there were only a few problems with legibility, and those were due mainly to occasional tears and some unfortunate taping in a few of the letters. When we were unable to decipher a word or passage we noted the fact in brackets, e.g. [illegible], and we used bracketed comments also when there were other textual problems like missing pages or questions about the sequence of pages or paragraphs. We have made minimal use of the [sic] device, especially leaving the children's spelling and grammar pure and uncluttered.

We have made a basic judgment about other explanatory information: Keep it simple. This decision is partly from principle and partly from necessity. As a matter of judgment, we believe the importance of the letters derives from the story they tell, and the story itself is pretty uncomplicated. We saw some danger in burying the letters under piles of footnotes and other documentation of remote or tangential relevance. Some minimum amount of footnoted explanation is helpful, though, and we tried to keep the number of references helpful and appropriate.

---

6 It is clear that Fannie wanted this story told. In the Draper-McClurg Family Papers folder for the 1920s (Western Historical Manuscript Collection, C3069, Folder 97), just a few years before Fannie died, there is a very rough fragment of an attempt, probably by Kate Draper, to write the story of the Dakota trip. (Kate and Emma lived on the farm with Fannie and Charlie until the parents died in the early 1930s, and continued living there the rest of their lives.) The fragment is a valiant attempt to fulfill the vision Fannie outlined in her February 1887 letter to Charlie, but it runs out of steam shortly after getting the expedition across the Missouri line into Kansas. Information in the fragment suggests that Arthur prepared an illustration for the story. His cartoon appears with Chapter I.

In some cases such valuable resources as newspapers were unavailable for the period involved, so some important topical references in the correspondence had to be left unexplained.

INCLUDED IN THIS FIRST CHAPTER *are letters written en route from the home in Lebanon, Missouri, to Walworth County, Dakota, and ending with the eruption occasioned by Fannie's disappointment upon arriving at the homestead. After traveling about 900 miles in a wagon with six children, she finds not only that her husband Charlie is not waiting there for them as promised but that the homestead is a disaster scene.*

The family had traveled from southwest Missouri west and north across Kansas to Nebraska and due north through Nebraska, crossing the Missouri River into Dakota Territory on the ferry at Running Water, Nebraska. We are not certain of the date of departure, though we know they left after the first week in June of 1886 and arrived at the homestead in mid-July.

Included in the party are Fannie McClurg Draper, the mother of Arthur (thirteen), Mame (twelve), Jim (ten), Joe (nine), Kate (four), and Emma (nicknamed "Johnny," just a year old and nursing). Fannie's father, Gov. J.W. McClurg leads the party, with the assistance of his son Joe and the driver, Mr. Lattimore. As the narrative develops, the mules, Pete and Alie (sometimes spelled Elie and sometimes Aleck) become important characters as well.

1

From Fannie Draper to Charlie Draper
Sunday, June 13, '86, Vista Station, MO, very near farm house

My Dearest Charlie:

It is now about three o'clock P.M. and we have just returned from the farm house (Mr. Dawson's) where we were invited to dinner and it was good. Mr. Dawson is an old homeguard man and served under Pa[1] whom he seems to think a greatdeal[2] of. Wherefore our dinner. Children enjoyed their spring and branch and it has been a pleasant change for us all. They have an organ and a girl who plays a little. I devoted the morning to washing dishes and straightening up and getting some of the dirt off myself and children by taking partial baths which made us feel a hundred percent better. It rained most of yesterday afternoon (and it was a little warm with sheet down but dry). It rained pretty hard just after getting here and at supper time so that I had to use the little stove which I liked very much. I made coffee and cooked some beef awhile in order to keep it for this morning and we enjoyed it for breakfast. We got it in Humansville. Of course the rain made mud for us and a general mess and consequently I did not feel the best in the world and would have given almost anything to have been at home but that did not last long and we are all feeling first rate. Little Emma is considerably tanned and wearies a good deal in the afternoons but is well. She is now crying and I must take her. I have nursed her and Joe is holding her near me but Mame is coming to take her as she cries with Joe. Jim and Kate and Joe

---

1 Governor McClurg had organized a home guard regiment in the early weeks of the Civil War. The regiment later became the Eighth Missouri State Militia Cavalry, which McClurg served as colonel.

2 Greatdeal is spelled as one word, and the family generally pronounced it with no gap between the syllables "gradeel."

now are looking at calves hitched behind a mover's wagon that has stopped to ask questions. Pa is not far away. I believe Arthur and Mr. Lattimer are watering mules and I believe the former intends bathing in the spring branch. Arthur walks about as much as he rides. All walk more or less. He has killed several birds with his gun and they have killed some with their flippers and all have been eaten. Jim killed a big frog this morning and gave Mame its legs. I know we are getting a long as nicely as we can and have been so blessed with good weather and I am feeling well and do not get so very tired and honestly believe it will agree with one, but altogether it is not pleasant yet there are parts that I enjoy. Let Mr. Johnson[3] carefully count expenses and if it does not fall too heavy advise him to send Em and children through on the train. Kate has just filled Emma's head with dirt—another job for me. I can't *begin* to keep a decent journal. I am just as busy as can be when we are not riding, with baby—cooking, washing dishes and sometimes "didy" and bed-making all being more laborious than when done at home. I commenced getting out bed-clothing and also tried to put them away but had to give that up to Mr. Lattimore & Arthur as it was too much for me. You know I sent a box back from Buffalo. You had packed everything so snugly that after getting a piece or two out it took me so long to get them back it wore my patience almost out and I thought the best thing to do was to make a little more room and it helped matters wonderfully. We saw Mr. Lovell Mrs. Roll & Fannie & Matt. Stopped with Mrs. Roll probably 2 hours but ate our dinner at the Niangua before reaching there. They gave us a little nice cake which we ate there and a bottle of mighty fine strawberries

---

3 Marshall Johnson, Fannie's brother-in-law and a former business partner of both her father and her husband, had persuaded the others to undertake the Dakota venture, based on his favorable experience there the previous year. The apparent plan was for the Johnson family, including their eight children, to follow the Drapers to Dakota in short order.

and a loaf of splendid light-bread to take along which we ate for supper. They were being hospitable and wanted us to stay all night and so did Mr. Lovell, but we thought best not. We have found good camping grounds and people stare and wonder when we tell them where we're going. I have bought some milk, butter, eggs but cannot always get those things when I try. Mr. L is now making fire and I will put on some fruit to cook. Mr. Lattimer has had breakfast ready two or three times by the time we get up. He is very willing and right good to do all he can. If you were just with us I might enjoy it. Little Kate talked a greatdeal about you the first day or two would almost cry but we would cheer her up. Mamie cried her self to sleep the first night we were out and I could have done so but said my prayers and went to sleep instead. I must help to get things together, as we have bedclothing and other things scattered all round and it is after 5 P.M. and we must have lunch. Emma is now asleep on wagon seat and Arthur sitting by to keep her on. Mame, Kate, Jim and Joe have all gone near the railroad to play. I am afraid I can only write you on Sundays and I will then have to write up my journal if I keep one It is just this way. Mr. Lattimer gets up and starts the fire and sometimes gets breakfast and pour out coffee and fix children's. Sometimes have to give baby attention before I eat. Then wash dishes hurriedly with Mame's help and pack them all so they can be packed in box without rattling. Get up nightclothing and wash and dress baby. Occasionally have a dirty didy to wash. Then I help to fold bed clothing and we all get in and start. When we stop at nights all hands are busy until we get to bed not a moment to spare for anything else. I will write when I can but I expect it can only be on Sundays unless we lay up on account of rains. I must now get Lunch. Goodbye old dearest. How I love you. Children send much love and many kisses. Kate is lying by me on a blanket asleep now. We ate the last of bread this morning and will open cracker box to night. Tell the folks the cake was so nice and we still have some of Em's cake and my cookies. We are within 4 miles of Osceloa. We intend to go the direct road from Osceola to Paola Kansas. We may go through Appleton City and we go to Lawrence from Paola. Hope to hear from you soon. Where are you boarding. Much love to all. Yours with lots of love.

Fannie

I am so glad you fixed envelopes for me. I may have more time next Sunday and hope to write a better letter.

From J.W. McClurg to Charlie Draper
Butler, Mo., 8½ a.m., Wednesday 16 June, 1886

All o.k. in every respect.
You write to Marshall.
Dear Friend,

All *very, very* well. All eat & sleep nicely. We have come 11 only this morning. 26 yesterday. We start for Paola, Ks., directly 45 miles. Then Lawrence. All send love.

J.W. McClurg

Inform Jimmie[4] where to write.

---

4 McClurg's son James, a dentist in Lebanon.

From Fannie Draper to Charlie Draper
Near Kansas line, June 17, 1886

My Dear Charlie,

Pa has just said that we can see Kansas. We struck Kansas 10 A.M. Thursday, June 19. I have not had a single chance to write since the above and that was done while on the way. It is now 10:20 A.M. and we are waiting for rain to stop or slacken so we can start. About 2 o'clock last night Mr. L. got up and secured the tent from rain. Near morning it commenced to rain and has been moderately so ever since. No leakages yet. I was the first around last night and did not sleep very well but feel pretty well today. Generally I sleep tolerably well. As you have asked the question in your two letters I answer it. How happy I was to receive your two good letters but the first made me shed a few tears (homesick) but no one knew it. We have had one little storm. Mr. L. woke us suddenly and said to get up quick and go to the house (about 150 yds. away) it was going to rain and blow hard. The tent was already flapping pretty hard boys were up and ready to go having slept in their clothes. Pa. M. & I hurriedly dressed then I wrapped baby and Kate in shawl and blanket and Pa advised to wait awhile as it was raining hard enough to wet us and said if it blew no harder the tent was the best place for us. The boys and little ones and Mame were soon asleep again. I lay down a little anxious but not frightened, and it did not last more than an hour any how. I was so glad Em & family were not along. I am sure they would have been very much frighted. Particularly Mag & Louise[5] and it would have been so miserable for all. *I do not* want them to come this way unless *it*

---

[5] Two of the younger Johnson children.

We are not sure when Arthur drew this cartoon but think it likely to have been prepared in the 1920s to accompany a narrative his sister Kate attempted but abandoned. Governor McClurg, of course, is the bearded old man on the left. Driving the wagon behind the mules, Pete and Alie, is McClurg's son Joe, and on the wagon bed are Fannie's daughters Mame and Emma. It's not clear which of the boys (Arthur, Jim, or Joe) are represented by the boys with bean flippers, though, as the bird implies, all of them were notorious for stalking birds with those weapons. Neighborhood children are seeing the travelers off, and neighbor ladies are planning to "expostulate" with Fannie about the advisability of the venture.

very essential. It is very hard. But do not be anxious nor uneasy for I am standing it right well. After lying in the wagon a few nights we went to the tent and like it better and a few nights ago we had tick filled with straw and that makes a more comfortable bed and it is so nice for children during the day as we put it between two back seats and it is much easier than riding on the seats and two can go to sleep as they frequently do after getting their play out. We all want to sleep in the afternoons and do a good deal of nodding. Some nights the baby sleeps splendidly and sometimes she nurses pretty often but that only disturbs me. Pa is so good & considerate for me. Mr. L is not first class help but we can get along with him. I do not like him neither does Pa. Last night I told him he ought to have consideration for others as well as himself and he said he meant to do what was right. He would neglect anything for a talk. The children are careful about mules and I hardly believe they would kick any how. They are very good and improving Pa thinks. Alie is made to do his share of the work and Pa looks after their interest all the time. They are duly admired every where. Mr. L. inquired price of such mules and the man said about $350 and would be worth $500 farther west. Mame is writing to her Grandma and will mail it here. Pa wrote a postal c. to Annie from Paola (for me). Kate and Emma are playing on the floor near me Kate singing tramp, tramp etc., Emma pulling at me when she can. Boys in barn near by. They have a good time and A. is sore walking so much and shirks where ever he can. Mame is always good. Bless her heart. I don't know what I would do without her. I forgot to say that the two first days I sat on the back seat & Mame insisted on my trying the one next the driver. I found it *so very much* easier I have been sitting there most of the time since. The back seat is used very little. The children all beg for a seat with driver each taking his turn. Occasionally two are there (back to back) with Pa & Mr. L. and Pa always exchanges with some of them in the afternoons. You asked about our cooking. Mr. L. generally helps *some* night and morning (simply because M and I cannot always do it) but we always wash up everything. It is all very tiresome on the back as we have to stoop so much. The table is fine. Could *not do without it.* We look after back part. All right yet. Emma sleeps a good deal and I carry her on a pillow. Children use the bolster either to sleep or ride on. We had terrible roads near Osceola. Saw Mr. Vawter and Jeb Chalfant there. The latter crossed the river with us. Business photography. Saw

Mrs. Lansdown & family at Butler. Tried very hard to make us stop a day. Lou is a mighty nice young lady. Mrs. L looks badly. None of the girls pretty. B is a beautiful town. I had no card from you there. Have received a No. of papers and two letters. One at Paola & papers. A & M almost quarreled over Youth's Companion but as Mame had C's[6] letter she gave way. Paola is a lovely town and has magnificent yards far ahead of Lebanon. I am taking items for Dakota. Some talk of starting & I will stop. Children send much love and many kisses to Papa. All miss Papa. This would be enjoyable with you. Emma opens her little mouth and kisses me every day for Papa, excepting Mame you were the first for a birthday kiss. Every body is so *very, very kind* to us that I cannot understand it. We suffer none with heat yet and feel that we are greatly blessed. Much love to all.

    Affy.,

    Fannie

We find portfolio and paper mighty handy & addressed envelopes also. Glad you went to church.

I hardly know what I have written but you can make allowances. Regards to inquiring friends. I hate to think of you being at home at nights. It is still raining some.

Expect to camp near Lawrence tonight and remain over Sunday 192 miles from home. We expect to pass through Holton and Seneca, Kansas and Pawnee City, Tecumseh, Lincoln, Columbus, Norfolk, Creighton, Nebraska. Running water at Missouri River crossing.

---

6 Clara Wallace, Mame's best friend in Lebanon. Clara was the only daughter of Judge W. I. Wallace, the model for the judge in Harold Bell Wright's *The Calling of Dan Matthews*. Clara died of tuberculosis as a young woman, and Mame contracted the disease from tending her best friend, according to the family stories. Mame, too, died young.

From J. W. McClurg to Charlie Draper
Lawrence, Ks, 10½ a.m., Monday 21st June, 1886

Dear Friend,

All well. No time to write more. We go by Holton, Ks. but by way of Topeka, for good road & no further. I presume the [illegible] named in Fannie's letter are correct ones. All doing nicely, *mules and all*. We came 212 miles.

We send love from all. Truly,
J.W. McClurg

From J. W. McClurg to Charlie Draper
Topeka. 12½ p.m. Tuesday, 22 Jun.

Friend

I received at Lawrence letters from Jimmie and Marsh[7] also.

You see above where we are, having stopped for lunch. We have come 12 miles to day. Roads heavy from rain last night. It was a good, gentle rain and was needed. We are all well; also mules and dog. The babe was somewhat unwell yesterday and early last night, but now all right. We get along nicely mules improving. We go to Holton from here N 28 miles. We have to go either directly N or directly W the roads running on Section Lines. I will see Bank at Holton as it may be last chance. I think

---

7 Marshall McClurg was J.W. McClurg's son.

we will make points named in Fannie's letter. I will try to [telegraph?] you from Holton.

J.W. McClurg

From J. W. McClurg to Charlie Draper
PRIVATE
Tecumseh, Neb. 3 p.m., 27 June 1886
CC Draper

Dear Friend

By 10 Aug. I will have to file papers for claim and pay fees at Land Office to Carter, Esq. I wish you to arrange for me to get sufficient money. Please see Mr. Johnson. If he can he will raise some on account of "Marshfield matter."[8] He will know what I refer to. I can't look for any from Jimmie for a while.

Truly & affy
J.W. McClurg

I will send soon, if not now, to you, the letter for R. & J. of course with pleasure.

[Note on back]
18 acres wheat
18" corn
7" corn or oats
6" oats
6" timothy

---

8 Jim McClurg had a dental practice in Marshfield, a town about 25 miles west of Lebanon.

5" pasture t[?]

Maria McDavid

¾ x ¼

Frank Swother

[Plus three diagrams that look like plans for planting crops.]

From Fannie Draper to Charlie Draper
[July 1886]

My Dearest Charlie:

I simply don't know what to say under my disappointment. Papa feels differently and will make it appear all right to you—but he is not a woman nor has he ever been able to appreciate one's situation, as good as he is. I am trying to day to wash him a handkerchief clean which he thinks is nothing at all—but with me it is hard work and next to an impossibility considering. I want to do what is right and am willing to stay here as long as you think best, but it is *simply dreadful.* You cannot begin to realize what it is like until you see it. And I wish you would take the time and not make a single purchase until you come and see for your-self. There is nothing in the neighborhood to eat but a few onions—and small ones. No provision store near, no potatoes, no nothing and every-thing desolate indeed. There is no water on our place as Terro caved the well in after leaving—also broke window from stable. I almost believe you would feel like throwing up the claim and never spend another cent on it if you should come and take a look. It will only take two extra days—and if you should buy things first and then not want to stay I don't think we could sell the things *at any price.* May be Joe would live at our house if we would set him up comfortably and stay until spring—but no that won't do—Well I don't know what we will do. If I were only stout and well and able to do but I am not and now my eyes are sore from wind and dirt and I am just looking worse than awfully and feeling bad enough. I don't want Annie nor any other woman or girl to come here. I know now that Em and her little girls will never come here and I am so glad that they are still in Lebanon. I am glad that Mr. J. still holds his farm and hope that he may always be able to. I will make out a memorandum of what I think we need and do as you think best about buying and having us stay here but I do wish you would first come and take a look. Pa don't know one thing and I do not believe it will pay us to stay. I wish you would come and see first. The boys (Joe & Thad) never want their Mama and the girls to come here and J. says he never means to bring Katie. It seems like forsaken country. There are no neighbors near enough to see from our home and Jodie and his folks are 5 or 6 miles away from us—entirely too far for us to *ever walk it*. The children are well and will have a good enough time. Mame will suffer some. I am sorry to have to write such a letter but I can't help it—it is so terrible and I am *not* homesick. If you want to you may be able to sell relinquishment to Mr. Lattimer.

From Charlie Draper to Fannie Draper
July 13, 1886

My Dear Fannie:

I have been so disappointed and you will be doubly so as it will come on you suddenly when you arrive in Walworth Co not to find me. I was counting on your former calculations as to time of arrival or would have been on my way now and I supposed you hurried after crossing the river thinking I would be there. Greenleaf[9] took sick in bed Saturday night and has been sick ever since or I would have left this morning. It is barely possible I will get away tonight or in the morning but I doubt it. Of course I can't leave with him in bed because Robin[10] can't sign drafts etc. and anyway has not had experience enough to leave him in charge. I will hurry through as fast as possible. I am afraid you will be terribly blue and discouraged to get there after the fire and find our house and place in such a dilapidated condition which I hoped to have fixed up before your arrival. Don't feel badly. I will be there soon. You had better go close to some neighbors where there is good water and camp till we can fix up our well or till I come and make other arrangements. You can have somebody do your washing and then just take things easy and rest and have patience. Dont try to do anything at the place. Things look blue but my salary will enable you to live all right if there are no crops and those Kansas people passed through worse times and see how they are fixed now. I staid at the farm last night all well but not so blue over Jodie's letter telling of the fire as you would expect.[11]

Have to put this in mail.

Love to all

Affy

Charlie

---

9 George H. Greenleaf, the president of the Laclede County Bank, where Charles was cashier.

10 A bookkeeper in the bank and nephew of Marshall Johnson.

11 No more information about the fire is available. It may have been a prairie fire that damaged both the Draper and the Johnson homesteads about 5 miles from each other. Or, there is suggestion elsewhere in the letters that the Johnsons were victims of arson at one point.

CHARLIE SPENT PART OF JULY *and most of August on the homestead, so there is only one August letter, which we include here with the September letters. We do not have a documented date for the arrival of the homesteaders at the place in Walworth County. Charlie's letter explaining his not being there to receive them is dated July 13th, but Fannie's "howler" written at the time of their arrival is undated. Charlie's notes say they moved in to the sod house on July 29th or 30th. It seems safe to assume that Fannie's party pitched the tent and stayed in that for awhile until Charlie got there. Details are not clear, but it is apparent that Charlie returned to Lebanon late in August.*

A lot of work was done on the house while Charlie was there, and the operation appears to be on an efficient footing by the time of his departure. Morale has vastly improved and the homestead is clicking along very happily. The letters are full of the rich detail of daily life on the homestead. Little glimmers of homesickness or loneliness for Charlie occur in Fannie's letters after he leaves and as time wears on, and there's some suggestion that Mame is missing her Lebanon friends, but life seems good—and if Charlie were there, life would be good indeed.

Marshall Johnson's letter of September 25th is worth some study as an astute and thoughtful analysis of the promises and risks of homesteading on the Great Plains. It all depends, he concludes, on ample and timely rains and faith in the promoters' slogan "Rain follows the plough." Hine and Faragher quote the old joke about a conversation between Mr. Westbound, who says of the Great Plains, "This would be fine country if we just had water," to which replied Mr. Eastbound, "Yes, and so would hell."[1]

Theodore Dak. [August] 27, 1886[2]

My Dearest Charlie:

This is only the 5th day since you left us but it seems a long time to me and I feel now as if I can never get used to the separation. I can't bear to talk of you at all and although I know it is very foolish yet I can't help it. I suppose I will overcome it sometime. And it makes me so homesick to see anything that you have worn. Kate and the boys are happy and always at play. Mame is not quite so reconciled. We had a rain last night and today it is rather cool to be comfortable—but fortunately it has driven away the mosquitoes which have been very troublesome indeed since you left. I spent almost one night in keeping them off of Emma. As soon as we get tacks we will cover frames for door and windows. The day you left I fixed pickled pork but it is a little sour and I am afraid will never be eaten. I have added more salt since and it may get all

---

1 Robert V. Hine and John Mack Faragher, *The American West: A New Interpretive History,* Yale University Press, New Haven and London, 2000, p. 337.

2 This is the only August letter. From notes of Charlie's, we know that he filed the homestead entry at Aberdeen on August 30, and we know from one of McClurg's letters that Charlie arrived back in Lebanon on or about September 3.

right. I am getting better and my rash has left me. I wish I had been well while you were here. I know it was so unpleasant for you when here. It makes me feel so badly. Joe has been pretty busy since you left. The well is done but the windlass. The old well is almost filled up and a place for the milk box dug. He has just put the latch on the door. He made a nice walk up this way from the well even with the top dirt around the well-- the top of it being stone. Arthur & Joe D. walked to Theodore[3] and back in 4 hours a few days ago. Arthur and Mame will probably go today. And as it is now about 2 o'clock and we want our letters to go it is time they were off. It was only 11 o'clock when we ate breakfast this morning. We have been losing so much sleep from mosquitos but I had been [illegible] to sleep again and Pa was taking catnaps during that time and let us all alone feeling that we needed the sleep. Joe is working at a shutter for our last window now. When you get this letter you will be at Lebanon I suppose. I hope you sold the mules & advantageously. I think of you most all the time. Love to Sallie and all the folks. Children join me in much love and kisses to you. Regards to Mr. Greenleaf.

Fannie

[Charlie to Fannie, undated. September 1886?]

. . . likely papa will return home. I wish Mag and Fannie[4] were there so Mame would have company. She would be so much more satisfied and so would you if Emma were there. I shaved [?] last night and

---

3 The village of Theodore, on the north bank of Swan Lake about 4 miles from the Draper homestead, existed from 1883 to 1803 only. In one two-story frame building, in addition to the post office, there was a general store, drug store, and hotel.

4 Mame's cousins, daughters of Marshall and Emma Johnson.

this morning after going to the PO and failing to get a letter from you little Tom[5] and I went to the Congregational Church. He sat bolt upright and as still as a mouse and if he was interested in the sermon it was more than I was. I had a slight cold which interfered with my hearing somewhat. Katie W. played the organ and the choir was composed of Mrs. S, Mrs. Wright, and Mrs. Joslin all sang soprano. I ought to go to choir meeting but there is little material to work on and I don't enjoy it as it is. The whole of the Greenleaf family were in their pew and Mr. & Mrs. Wallace but I did not see Clara. The little Wright girls I noticed and Mrs. Kirk, Mrs. Faulkner, besides the regular old stand bys. Mary has had fever since last Tuesday and the doctor has been here a number of times. I don't think there is anything at all serious but Sallie has been somewhat alarmed. She seems about cool tonight and I think will be nearly well by tomorrow. That is how I got my cold, sitting up and holding her the other night from 11 to 1 o'clock so Sallie could get some sleep. The others are all well. Jim came back from his Richland trip feeling very badly with sick headache, but he is about well again and has been busy I believe. His trip was not very successful but he said patients came in after he was packed up. He felt too badly to unpack for them and will take them in next time. Hoot [?] is still here but seems to be doing little if anything. I hope Jim will do well this winter. Everything is progressing about as usual at the farm. All well and Frank uptown early in the morning. None of you have written anything about our [illegible] contest so I don't know what is being done. I wrote the Gov a few days ago and enclosed $15.00 but I am afraid he will not get it in time—still he may. I will not send a draft in this as we are short of NY exchange but will send it during the week. Don't hesitate to let me know when you

5 Tom Monroe, son of Sallie, Fannie's sister.

The approximate site of the Draper homestead in Walworth County. No remnants of the soddy, well, stable, or any other signs of the Drapers' homestead can be found, and the "evidence" for taking the picture as it appears is the following information from Charlie as he is imagining in one letter (October 17) as he looked off toward Theodore and Swan Lake: "I can remember just how," Charlie writes, "our mules look coming over the hills from Theodore and I can imagine myself standing at the cabin door with you and the children watching first the mules' ears and then their heads and then the Governor in the wagon." The photographer took a picture of a spot in the distance looking from the Draper property toward Swan Lake.

want more money for I did not put you up there to starve or freeze. You ought to get in at least 3 tons of coal right away, I think, and a good supply of provisions so nobody would be compelled to go to RR in bad weather. Let me know how much to send you. If you did not get flannel to suit you at Bowdle I can send you red factory flannel that will cost there not exceeding 35 cents a yard. Or I can get Sallie to make underclothing of it for any of you and send by mail. Don't Joe and the Gov need some flannel undershirts and drawers? And don't all of you need flannel underclothes? Would factory flannel be too coarse? It is said to last splendidly.

I believe I wrote you that Mother and Fannie were keeping house for Arthur.[6]

I will get Annie to send you that medicine before long. You said you almost live on my letters. That is the way it has been to me. You had . . . [Remainder of the letter is missing]

Walworth Co. Dakota. Monday 1 p.m., 6 Sept. 1886
CC Draper

Dear Friend,

I calculate you arrived at Lebanon friday 3d Inst. and have recovered from your "Dakota chills" and wrote to Fannie a long letter on the 5th (Sunday you know) and probably one to me. I think you are *yourself* once more. All here *are themselves now* and have been for some time, having no more chills to contend with. Fannie would be perfectly satisfied if you were here and thinks it would be foolish now to give up. Arthur is falling in love with Dakota. Fannie talks about *nice walks* and nice *drives* (that could be), etc. If we have good crops next year and the winter not so severe as some represented when in Mo. you would have to use a stick to drive them away. If we have to keep the mules we will add to the convenience and make them more than pay. If unsold, we expect to arrange to use Mr. Will's sulky plow and I expect to backset your present plow-

---

6 Fannie is CC's sister; Arthur is CC's brother in Colorado.

ing and Mr. Johnson's and Jodie's,[7] and in the spring to turn sods, getting a third horse or mule to use.

Today Jodie started to see Barber with mules and wagon, with full instructions. If he don't sell, he will return by Bowdle[8] and bring sash.

Today the wind is from W. of N. and cool, but not cold. Should it clear up before night, as I think it will, we will likely have frost in low places. Saturday, 3d, we got cow over and calf "snow flake" alias "crip." Both are larietted and on good grass. Of course we will fix up stable in due time, get hay & [illegible] if mules are unsold, we will enlarge upon it. We can plan for hay.

You will, of course, give me land-office news. I begin to think that persons residing out of Dakota cannot tree-claim in it. Joe will have Number, so as to pre-empt in a few days [illegible] is vacant. Tell Sallie that Fannie will write—but when? Also, that I intend but will not hasten much as she will hear from you and Jimmie all the news. I look now for a letter from Jimmie—after return from Waynesville.

Your children began school this a.m. I am writing in tent and sleep there. Joe is cutting grass to-day in Jodie's place.

We begin to need the hay barn. But Sept, Oct., and Nov. we expect to mainly be pleasant. Hoping all are well as we are. We send all much love.

Truly & affect.
J.W. McClurg

---

7 Marshall and his sons Jodie and Thad had homesteads about 4 or 5 miles from the Drapers' place.

8 Bowdle was the market and (later that fall, railroad town) nearest the Draper homestead—about 15 miles north in Edmunds County.

_____

Walworth County, Dakota, 9th Sept. 86
6 ¼ in the morning, before you are up.
CC Draper

Dear Friend,

You see I am an early bird and writing this in the tent; that it is somewhat cool, the wind uneven from the south and in an hour or two it will be quite pleasant. Such now is the weather here.

Fannie is up—All are *very well. Joe will soon milk.* Fannie did first churning last evening. Jodie Johnson got back at dusk evening of 7th. He accomplished nothing but at no expense, except loss of time, as the carter did not want to buy a team having four teams now. It was a mistake. Yesterday I walked over to see Brumberg, he having returned, Joe McC with me to see him on other business. I believe he will buy. I priced him mules & harness, cash $350 and a cow that later he could have sold for $65, worth now, I suppose, $50. He told me to take over the mules this a.m. and to look at the cow. I think therefore he will buy. He may not.

I expect to go to the P.O. same trip, and I will add a P.S. before sealing this.

The tree contract is set for 28 Oct. Joe and I are arranging papers and will soon return same to J.S. Carter, Jr.

Joe put sash in both windows yesterday. He goes next to plastering.

I write hurriedly. Jodie is cutting grass. We need that coal, wood and hay stove, but are not freezing.

Write about the claim south of Jim & Terro's. What do your sisters think?[9] Now is the time to secure lands.

Much love to all.

Truy & affy

JW McClurg

We will take wagon and team and Fannie & Emma will go also and to P.O. for molasses, flour etc., which do not come by mail but we expect some mail also and mail this to go by mail tomorrow morning. Fannie can see cow. I will add a P.S., as we will go by Brunberg's.

Please deliver Jimmie's letter to him. I am out of envelopes.

---

11 ¼ a.m. at Theodore

Fannie with Emma are there. Mr. and Mrs. Brunberg also. I think we will sell possibly wagon to him but if so will have to keep a good note, sell on time with interest for us. I will write.

JWMc

---

11 ¼ a.m. Friday 10 September 1886
CC Draper

Dear Friend

This may go tomorrow by Jodie to Bowdle or it may not start until Monday morning 13, as Jodie may get a draft this evening from his

---

9 McClurg refers to Charlie's sisters' interest, apparently, in homesteading in Dakota. His sisters Fannie and Laura did attempt homesteading in Colorado at one point.

father. If not he goes to Bowdle tomorrow with a beef steer to sell. I think he will hear from his father this evening, and we from you.

Well—as to the mules. A sale was not made yesterday. I presume one will not be made. Brumberg evidently wants the mules. From his actions and remarks. I had but little about his buying yesterday and the wagon too at the figures I had made him. But he at last refused to come to them and offered to buy on terms that I could not accept. Fannie agreed with me. He may come to our terms, but I think not. I think the greatest trouble with him is that he has not money enough. He has a good milk cow (and Fannie likes her looks and she gives now 5 gals. per day; they say 6) part Durham, red and good large size that is worth now $50—lately $65. I offered to take the cow and $350 cash for mules and harness. He then asked me if we would take a good note secure and endorsed by him, for $125 and 10% interest from date, due 1 November, 1887, with now about 3 mos. interest accrued. After consulting Fannie, we concluded to take it—making 225 cash and the 125 note and cow (she has no calf, having lost it). He then spoke of buying the wagon, cover and all. I told him the lowest figures were $54 or 55$ cash. He then asked if we would take another cow also. I at last told him after looking at another good cow, part Jersey, not so large as other cow, giving 3 gals. per day, that we would, and as he was reluctant, told him to drive over the cows and pay 225 cash and note 125 and drive back home the mules, with harness and wagon and cover, all complete. He reluctantly declined and wanted the whole complete at $400, the 2 cows to go in and they and 125 note and $175 cash to make the $400. I believe he would add $25 cash if he had it. I am sure he has not the money. His wife said so to Fannie several times & I heard her say it. I thought you did not want a sale that would give cash, now, only 175, especially so if you can manage the cash part at Lebanon and have the benefit of the higher value next spring. And the service this fall in breaking old land and in spring turning sod. We can get (now promised) Mr. Hill's sulky plow and I can turn sod when the time comes, getting a 3d mule or horse. The old ground can be broken by them along with ordinary walking plow. We can get hay for breaking.

These particulars I give as you may wish to change your instructions!

All are well. Today is pleasant with wind from NW clear and cool. The wind turned round about noon yesterday and came from NW. We have pleasant days and cool nights, nice for sleeping. Musquitoes troubled a little for a few nights only. I sleep in tent and am now writing in it and very comfortable. As to my views and feelings—I like the prospects here more and more every day. The capabilities of the country are great; its possibilities great and probabilities just about as great. We are bound to have R. Roads near us.[10] The Road to Bowdle is constructed and in a few days freight etc. will be run to that point. That is only 18 miles from here and the other road, when to Gettisberg will be no further. But they will be nearer in a year or two. Let next year be a good crop year here (I think it will be) and things will buzz. Now is the time to secure lands. Also the time to put in cultivation all that it is possible to.

Much love to all

Truly & affecty

JW McClurg

Mamie goes to P.O. with me.

All are well.

---

10 Sometime later, the Minneapolis St. Louis Railroad passed just by the Draper homestead. The road bed is still visible.

Theodore, Sept. 10, 1886

My Ever Dear Charlie:

When I want to write some one else has the ink. Pa is now using it. And as he will tell you what our mule trade (I was with him yesterday) amounted to, I will pass it over. Brunberg had a nice cow that I should like to have gotten and if he can only raise the money I believe he will come to our terms and willingly. Our children began their studies with eager interest on Monday knowing the Lebanon school commenced then, and they were full of talk concerning what other children of their acquaintance might be doing at that time. They have kept it up nicely this week and are now out having a recess. Emma is asleep. Pa in tent writing and poor Joe almost helpless with lame back. He wrenched his back some way just in picking up loose hay and throwing it into wagon. Probably has taken some cold also. He wanted to haul for plastering but I presume wont be able before Monday any how. Jodie wanted him to go to Bowdle and help him drive steer tomorrow but I suppose he will hardly be able. I lent Jodie $1.40 a few days ago but I suppose he will return it when he gets money. If he gets money from home today he will go away tomorrow. I feel real sorry for Jodie—and the boy is ragged too. I mended his pants while on him this morning and put on a button for him before he went to Cookingham's.

There is so much uncertainty about selling mules that you had better send money to pay the Hulls and a little to me also (if you can manage it). When I can send the stove to Ipswich and get machine I must commence my winter sewing and will have some goods to buy—I must either get the boys each a heavy pr. of pans or the material and make them. And get some flannel for underwear and a dress for Kate, Mame & myself of flannel or something as warm. Our mornings and evenings are quite cool now and I do not want cold weather to catch us unprepared. So far this month compares with our cool Oct. days at home. But I like it very much. Coming from Theodore yesterday it was some chilly with my shawl on, but it was cloudy and quite windy. I spent $5.00 for flour, sugar, coffee, soda, molasses, and a box of yeast cakes. I still have more than a dollar left. Although the cow gives a small quantity of milk, it helps out wonderfully. Kate has her tea kettle tea again and the children milk for the coffee also the rest of us. Mame her glass—(as she had to give up tea and coffee on account of headache) and I have a little for gravy too.

Then it would do you good to see Pa drink the buttermilk. He drank a glass at breakfast this morning before eating a bite. You see we are not starving. And when you can be with us we will not want to give up our Dakota home.

Taking care of the milk is quite a "diversion" for me. It is a pleasure. I have washed parts of two days of this week not being quite able to put in full days and do other work satisfactorily. I am getting the work arranged more and more systematically all the time and it is becoming more pleasant. The windows keep out more of the dirt and our house is quite comfortable even mornings and evenings. Still we must get the other stove when we can. Yesterday, I went into Mrs. Brunberg's house and things were in such an awful condition that it made our own little sod house feel more like home than ever and I was glad to get back to it. Mr. McCleveland told me a day or two since that his wife talked every day of coming down but different things hindered her. The children have been off gathering stones and found some rather pretty ones. They all seem happy and contented. It seems to me that Arthur ought to have some other study this winter to take the place of Physical Geography which I think he can get through with by that time.

If Robin doesn't care for parting with one of his plain copies in his compendium I wish you would send it to me and I can make good use of it. I will see Jodie, I believe he had one, but I suppose it is at home. I wish you could see Emma walk. She seldom crawls now and will walk quite a distance from the house.

Is there any chance of selling to Charlie Smith? I was so sorry to hear of Mr. Hall's death and feel so sorry for his wife. Poor girl, I suppose she will hardly want to marry again. And poor Lucy Ellis. Do you know what her condition is financially? And will she remain at Linn Creek? Pa will go to Theodore this evening with Mame and some of the other children. I can't spare them all.

I am fully expecting a letter from you. Your first since reaching home. A week seems like a long time to wait. Today is Friday and this letter will not go out until Monday. I want to write to Sallie soon. Much love and many kisses to all loved ones. How I should love to see Em, Sallie[11] and their flocks. Love to Miss Mary whom I should also love to see.

Affy—

Fannie D

Ipswich, Dak., 11 ½ a.m., Friday 17, Sept, 1886
CC Draper

Dear Friend,

In haste. I soon start for home with wagon, team and supplies. We all thought that the cold was liable to be such that we should make haste

---

11 Emma McClurg Johnson and Sallie McClurg Monroe are Fannie's sisters.

to exchange of stoves etc., and other supplies. They acted very well as to stoves. I take back the one (like it) priced to you at $15 or 16$. I have bought some groceries etc. from Jewett Bros. I have drawn on you to order of *Bank for $25.* Fannie thought best to do this rather than wait. I will write at length from home and give you all particulars as to stove exchange, etc. etc.

I mail to you with this a letter from Fannie. Tell Jimmie and others that I will probably not write from here. But soon after getting home where I expect to be Saturday. I left 15th. All were well. We had some rain that day—not much. Then colder, but not very. It is now cool and pleasant.

I rather think that hereafter we will do business at Bowdle. Trains are running there now—and shortly it will be regular and heavy articles will be about as cheap there as here.

I am very well—we brought through 50 bu wheat for Cartwright. He goes on to Chicago. I return alone. Much love to all.

Truly etc.

JW McClurg

I take also supplies for Mr. Johnson. His truck has gone on to Bowdle. I will get it there, etc.

Theodore, Sep. 18, 1886

My Ever Dear Husband,

It is early Saturday morning and no one else is astir. Oatmeal is cooking away on my little coal oil stove and I want to write you before breakfast if I can as I have a busy day before me. We look for Pa today and then can have a stove again. It is pretty cold up here and fire will be very acceptable and pleasant —still we have not suffered and yet yesterday morning after the sun had risen Joe brought ice to the house on that old bucket kept at watering well and the part right in contact with sides of bucket was ¼ inch thick in ice. We have had a few heavy frosts. I want your advice about having plowing done. Will it pay to get another man with money so scarce? Joe is now entirely disabled with his back and we cannot tell how long he may remain so and time waits for no one. We will probably have to pay $2½ per acre at least and hands very scarce. I might be able to get Bumberg either by day or month but don't know. Several times Pa has said he would or really intended borrowing a sulky plow and going to work himself and said he would like it. Nothing has been done about plastering yet and I think we ought to wait on Joe as long as weather will allow. And then other things must be done before cold weather is on us. Manure hauled away and stable in good condition for cows and mule. Hay gotten up. In a few days, Joe may be all right and probably will as I have known these spells to last him on the farm several weeks. I am sometimes afraid it might terminate in rheumatism. The plowing you know can be left until spring with the exception of garden and the piece sown in oats which can be plowed so easily after spreading manure over the former. Do not worry about these matters and rather than incur an additional debt let them alone and all may still be done. I have just thought that someone might do it for the use of the mules in exchange. Do not write to Pa to have these things done unless you have plenty of money and I know you haven't. You know he is only economical when business is concerned I mean where he can save on himself. If he thinks you can raise money somehow for such purposes, he will go ahead and hire a great deal. Burn this letter when you read it. I took the baby and Joe and walked over to Mrs. Keerchoff for bread yesterday. Arthur and Mame had gone over before but it interfered so greatly with their lessons that I did not want to send them and Joe was not able. Kate is very much interested in her books at present but I suppose it will not last long. The boys' principal sport now is gigging spring frogs—and they kill quite a number. They use a lath with something pointed in the end. I have some legs to cook for them this morning. Emma is crying. Joe gone to milk (He has not given that up yet) so I will finish breakfast. Goodbye you old darling. If awake the children would join me in much love and many kisses to their "good old Papa." Also love and kisses to all homesick [sick is lined out] folks who are too numerous to mention but we think of each one—separate, often and often.

Affy, Fannie

Remember me to all inquiring friends.

I was forgetting to make a memorandum of what things we will need this winter but will enclose one as nearly as I can of what things I believe we will absolutely need. In addition to my mind if they are not too expensive I want to get 8 light blankets for sheets. They will be warm and save washing. If I find them too costly I will not buy but may be able to get something else (not cotton) to answer as well or better. Joe intends using a part of the $10 for underclothing when he gets it. I found out by asking him. We will go to Bowdle and back today to do my purchasing. Yours with lots of love, Fannie

Box of crackers—sugar, Broom. Chamber. Stove. Washing machine and one tub. If not too costly. If so—two tubs and a wash board and boiler. Magnetic soap, as it is spendid. Red cross lye for making soap as it will use up meat skins—or the Red Seal if cannot get the other and Lewis lye if you cannot get either of the other kind. If only one bake pan comes with stove get two smaller ones. One steamer. A vessel of somekind of wear for baking beans. Something thick as tin does not do well. Jodie thinks we should get a stove that will burn either wood or coal. A young lady told me that gasoline was much cheaper than wood and it may be better to get a gasoline cooking stove and a coal for heating. I really don't know what is best to do. We want a water bucket. Get one common chair that we can have rockers put to. Joe can do that. I do wish we had never heard of Dakota. I think. O if only we could only manage to get that Greenstreet property [illegible] how nice it would be. And he could so easily sell it cheap if he would but it wouldn't do any good to talk about it. [illegible] days longer and [illegible] before doing anything [illegible] as you may require it. Love & kisses [illegible] hoping to see you very soon.

Affy, Fannie

I don't believe I would like Jodie's stove. Don't get the Burdett Smith & Co. whatever you do. I will try my best to abide by your decision but it makes me feel terrible to think of staying. I am actually afraid of suffering this winter. We will want some kind of churn if we stay. There is so much danger of freezing and breaking, get a wooden one and two buckets or pans for putting milk in.

I received a letter and package of plum seeds from Annie yesterday. I love to read your letters over and over again and I hope you will still be cheerful and happy and we will do our best to help along. Pa is well and I believe enjoyed his trip although it rained more or less while he was on the way and it was cold but he had no particular trouble and he did not seem unusually tired. Good bye old dearest I must get supper, which is dinner, too.

The sun is bright again and all want to be out.

With love,

Fannie

I may need a dol. or two for incidental—Thread, buttons, &. I will be as economical as I can. Fannie.

Mame wants you to be sure and send any fashion books that come to Lebanon for us.

Pa will write to Jim Monday.

My Dearest Charlie,

It is Sunday afternoon. My letter has not gone to Theodore yet but Mr. Johnson intends going over this afternoon to take letters. The mail never goes from Theodore Saturdays and Sundays anyhow. Pa got in early last night. All ok. Brought #16 stove back which I am sure I will like. They only made a deduction of $2 on the stove. Mr. Johnson & Jodie stayed with us last night, as they came in rather late, and it was too cold and cloudy for them to go on. We had an apple feast at our house last night and what a good time we had. The children, of course, as happy as could be. Kate was asleep but was ready for a big share this morning and commenced before breakfast. Mr. J. and Jodie slept with Kate and Mame with Emma and me. I did not sleep very well between Mame and apples but feel pretty well to day. Mr. J., Jodie, and Joe got up before I did and put up the stove in time to get a late breakfast. I mean they commenced the work before I got up. Pa took the gasoline tank back but I don't know how they settled that. He will give me particulars tomorrow. I am so happy to have a heating stove and one that I can bake with. I received your good long letter of the 12 and 25 dols. in draft. So don't bother about my [illegible] and do not send more money until you know we want it. Pa has just told me he has $5 or more in his pocket for me.

"The Wayside" Near Theodore, Sept. 23, [1886]

My Dear Charlie:

Pa returned from Bowdle yesterday with lumber for storm door etc. Jim went along and had a good time. Today is colder and drizzling rain in the morning but almost clear in the afternoon. Pa & A. will go to Theodore in a few minutes. Joe is daubing preparatory to plastering. Mr. J. & Jodie have borrowed wagon and gone for wood, so Pa & A. will ride the mules. Jim & Joe are after frogs. Kate is out and Mame at her History. Studying does not agree very well with Mame. Much love to one and all—

Affy—

Fannie D.

Theodore Dak. Sept 25th 1886

Dear Charley:

We have just returned from the hay field, at the close of our day's work and are now at your house waiting for the Gov's return from Bowdle. We expect him to bring our wagon which was there for repairs. He will also bring the mail from Theodore. We all expect letters from home. Have just been to supper with all at the table and pretty well. Mame is complaining some, but nothing serious the matter is "about" helping her mother. Fannie is looking first rate and feeling equally well but has been hard at work all day and feels tired. Dakota is a place for work—activity—but the surroundings here seem to impart the ability. My first impressions of Dakota are unchanged. There seems to be here every element of a boundless prosperity except the required moisture. This must be God-given, as it is to most agricultural countries. I can't see how general irrigation is possible. But if God gives us plenty of rain at the proper season I do believe we can, in all the leading agricultural crops, except corn, double Missouri, and with much less labor and expense. And with these rains the grasses will grow and the stock business as compared with other states will be equally profitable. These are my impressions. But these rains may not be given; but some how I feel like they will. This fertile land with general salubrious climate was not & is not intended for a waste—a wilderness—and some way or other this question will be solved favorable to the prosperity of the country. I don't fear the winters—whether in their severity or length. East of us in same latitude the winters are more severe than here yet the people are happy very prosperous and develop the highest type of manhood then why should we fear the winters here. We can provide against their rigors and prepare for their length.

I had gotten thus far when the Gov. arrived and took our wagon and traps and started for home.

26th

Today we took dinner at Cookinghams. Took them a few of our green apples and a sample of evaporated fruit. Spent an hour or two in pleasant chat and am again at home reading and writing etc. The weather is pleasant—not cold and generally clear but is often too windy to suit me exactly. In the low grounds there has been considerable frost and one morning last week at your house they had ice ¼ in. thick but we have had no frost here though some nights have seemed cold enough for it. At Mr. Tanners vegetables are still growing untouched by frost.

We see wolves every few days, as we go to and from work and one came near us in the hay field. Yesterday as we went to work about half way between Mr. Tanners and your house Jodie shot a grouse with his pistol. It flew 250 or 300 yds and fell. Jodie started to get it, but it seems a large black wolf was watching and saw the bird fall and shot like an arrow from a point some 200 yds to Jodie's left beat him to the grouse of course & carried it off much to Jodie's surprise and disgust. I sat in the wagon an interested spectator and when Jodie returned another large wolf was in the rear of the wagon. (Don't mean in the wagon but on the prairie over which we had just passed). He galloped off & went his way. This was about 7:30 a.m. Don't you think they are bold? The burning of the prairies may have made their means of subsistence more precarious, forced them into the settlements while there may be no danger yet through abundance of caution. Fannie will see that the children are not exposed. I would like to have a long range rifle for the benefit of the ugly beasts.

We are nearly through haying. Have at the stack near 150 tons. May get some more from Terro—in same flat with ours & put up this week. If we don't need it for our stock we think it will command a fair price before spring. We will have the matter in view and it is possible we may do some thing at baling & selling hay another year. With proper effort I think we may secure considerable that we could put on the market at small cost. I wish you could see Clough as to the cost of baling, the price and capacity of a machine for the purpose, and the force—men & horses necessary to run it and write to me. Don't mention the matter so as to disclose what we have in view.

The correspondence with Everett I may or may not have explained to you. It occurred while you were in Dakota. The matter should perhaps have attention. Everett sent $435 in settlement of his note. Mr. Greenleaf upon reflection directed me to say to him to execute, have recorded and sent to him (Greenleaf) quit claim deed to the land purchased at tax sales and he could surrender Everett's note. Everett replied he would do so but said there were taxes due on the land sold him at the time of the sale which he wanted Mr. G. to first pay. I told him whatever was due on this a/c at time of sale, would be paid. I understood that you had looked up the tax matter—had indeed paid the taxes and therefore did nothing, not even calling Mr. Greenleaf's attention to it, only to say I would refer the matter to you on your return. Can you give it attention?

I don't know how long I may be here. Perhaps a month or so yet. We have got breaking to do, then the sheds, stables and house to build, if weather and means permit.

Should you see our folks tell them I will write again within a day or two.

Cattle are doing well. Grass and water good. We must herd the summer half of the year but think we can get enough to herd for others to pay this expense. Nearly every settler has a few cattle—from 2 or 3 to 30 or 40 head, but not enough to justify a herder. These we will take into our herd at about $1.00 per head.

Hope you are all well and things prospering at home.

Write when you can.

Very truly your friend.

M.W. Johnson[12]

---

12 Marshall Johnson was Emma McClurg's husband, CC Draper's brother-in-law.

The Wayside, Near Theodore. Sept. 27, 1886

My Ever Dear husband:

What wouldn't I give to see you this bright afternoon for I am lonely and worried. I do not have many such days, but in spite of everything they will sometimes come and then I think O if Charlie was only here. Today I feel as if I could not stay here this winter. But tomorrow I know I shall feel differently. One fall month is almost gone and although situated as we are time sometimes seems tedious I know there is an end and it can't be very long before we shall have spring and after a good visit from my own dearest I shall try to make up my mind to stay longer if it is best. Joe is still at work in the house. He is now at the trap door—which he has to fit before proceeding with plastering. He is very slow indeed. But I think is doing a good job. We are all in a muss of course and these cool days we are crowded together in a small space with confusion all around. Mamie has read *Little Women* with a radiant countenance—for I believe I never looked at her that she was not smiling when reading it—and now she is reading it to Arthur. I am so glad you sent it as she has not been well for awhile but is almost herself again now. I believe I never saw a child enjoy a book as she does this one. Arthur is getting his geography now. I have selected the most difficult parts for him and I find he has to study more than I first thought. But he could easily take another study, although he hates most terribly to apply himself. And I have more trouble in getting him to study than any of the others. Pa was telling me this morning that Saturday on his way to Bowdle he was surprised to hear Arthur's store of information about birds, grasshoppers, etc. Said he talked a long time and a greatdeal about such things with interest and intelligence which interested him. I am afraid I cannot get suitable goods here for winter clothing. Pa brought me samples from two stores in Bowdle and all were light flannels but there were three other stores he did not try. Their prices were high. I shall probably go. If it were not for the cost of getting things here I would have you get heavy flannel from the Factory and if Sally could, get her to make a dress each for myself, Mame and Kate. She could make them plain as we would wear them all the time. They keep ready made clothing of some kind at Bowdle and I will see if I can get pants for the boys when I go. Pa sold $4.00 or more for Joe which he will replace when Joe gets his money. Joe sent his application for preemption a few days ago but he very much fears now that others were ahead of him and he will not get the claim. In that case he will listen to other suggestions from you and be glad. Geo. Terro asks $200 for his place. Joe Terro died a few days ago at Aberdeen.

Sept. 28

My Dear boy I am feeling much better today but want to see you just as bad. Your good long letter of 20 made me feel so happy last night. You see it was seven days on the way. Pa and Arthur went after mail last evening and Jodie and Mr. J. took supper with us but we had eaten when the former returned for it was after dark. And Mr. J., Joe, Pa, Mame and I got letters from home and what a happy jolly group we were around the table—each one so happy in his own letter. Mame and Arthur delighted over the former's letter from Clara. Mame loves C. dearly. I am so busy today but have just been aching to read your letter again. It was so good and comforting. Pa received the other draft of $251 and will pay the Hulls. I will also give Joe some. You are so good and kind to want to have our dresses made for us and although I had thought of putting it off until after my Bowdle trip—it will be such a help to me (as I suppose Sally has offered to make them). I will get you to please have it done. But I will have no knitting done until I see what yarn can be bou't for here. We shall go next week if weather is pleasant. Sallie will know what quantity of flannel to get and the factory flannel and consult her own taste and I will be satisfied. I will send the length of Mame's sleeves and mine must be two inches longer at least. Also the length of her dress in the back from neck band to the hem inclusive. Sallie will know the length to make mine from her own. The dutch blue she made me is lots large and I believe she made it just by her pattern unless she has a plain pattern that she prefers I would like to have it made as she did the blue with a long waist. Mame has grown some and if Mag has a 13 year old pattern Sallie may please make by it. I think Mag has a jersey probably that size or some plain pattern. Mary's size will do for Kate. And I would like to have one for Emma too. Let us know about the time she will expect to send them and we may be able to make it convenient to go to Bowdle. I will ascertain soon if Express Co. carries goods to Bowdle on trains and will write you. It is real cool today and stove is all ok and house warm and will soon be snug. Joe is now making cupboards. He has put pegs in the wall for the shelves and their cleats about all the room we could spare for such things and I think all we will particularly need. Joe carried and packed other things in the tent box today so he could use the last large box for cupboard. The boys' latest amusement is bow and arrows and they can get fun out of any thing. All were pleased with the card you sent them and had a big laugh over "Uncle Joe's" particularly. Pa is impatient to get off and it makes me forget what I want to say. I believe little Emma has Xzemus,[13] as her little stomach is broken out and she scratches it ter-

---

13 Eczema?

ribly. I am afraid of getting it. Emma does not feel entirely well but gets out doors every chance she gets. Kate is always happy and generally good. The children love you too dearly to ever forget you. When you write again say something about our returning in the spring for Mame's sake. She watches for it, in all of your letters. Poor child she will have the blues at times. I must write you a better letter soon. I have written in such haste. Send me a fine pointed pen. Excuse mistakes. With lots and heaps of love for one and all both great and small, I am yours, etc., etc. Children often kiss me for Papa and love dearly talk of you. Jim never kisses me good night without kissing his hand in the direction of Lebanon and saying good night Papa. If you had seen my dido over your old coat a few days ago—you would have either laughed or cried. Kate is by me singing to herself. M is reading, baby tearing paper—Pa and Joe getting mules ready to take letters to Theodore and boys out at play. Old Em. Johnson came over and offered me some "buttah"[14] at last. If you had only been here I might have accepted

Good bye my old dearest,

Yours Fannie

Sept. 29, 1886

Dear Fannie:

I have time only for a note in the midst of business and will write you a letter on Sunday as usual. Tom had a flannel shirt & a pair of long big stockings that he would not use again and asked me whether the boys

---

14 Probably Andrew Johnson, a neighbor who lived about a mile from the Draper homestead, and, apparently, amused the Drapers considerably. There are several references to Mr. Johnson's "buttah."

would like to have them and I said yes. So I send them by mail today, and Arthur's gun pin is in an envelope in one of the socks. Joe can see how to screw it in by examining it. Tell Arthur he will have to keep watch that it don't get loose again. I wouldn't spend a dollar on breaking ground this fall. As Joe feels able during the fall he can probably break up the garden good and deep and also break the 10 acres on the hill so it can be put into wheat but it is too late to break sod profitably and if it wasn't we can't raise the money to do it. So I would wait until spring for sod breaking. Was glad to see from your letter to Sallie that Uncle J. likes our mules. They are as Charley Johnson would say "yaller good uns." Give our love to all and kiss the little ones. Would like to write you a long letter but must wait till Sunday. Your letters are always most welcome and interesting.

Good bye,

Affy.,

Charlie

I have done nothing as to clothes and will wait for instructions from you when you answer my letter on the subject.

Robin sends love to all of you.

I want to hear *good reports* from that gun. Tell me how your stove works and what you did about vessels.

———————————

[Shopping list sent to CC in Fall of 1886?]

Stockings for child:

Arthur supplied.

Yarn for J.J. 2 lbs 60 —$7.20

knitting same———— .80

420
South Street,

Mc Millan,

Springfield,
Mo.

*Joseph W. McClurg as he appeared in the mid-1890s when he served as the head
of the Federal Land Office in Springfield, Missouri—approximately ten years
after the winter in the Dakota Territory.*

Stockings for M & self

2 prs each 50 cts. 2.00

Heavy pair pants for A. 2.00

Flannel for Kate's

underwear for A. 4 yds 2.00

M. Jim & Joe supplied

Flannel for Kate's

underwear, 3 yds.,......1.20

2 undervests

Flannel for myself

for underwear or if

cheaper buy undervests 3.50

Flannel dresses for M. Kate & Emma 4.50

I can get along without one. My little brown jacket I can wear as a house sack and I won't need the dress. M's and my shoes will probably cost 2.00 apiece (maybe not) and the others some lower. Kate has a new pr. of light shoes. And I will only get her a pr of arctics.

Baby has her booties which I think will do for winter.

[Fannie to CC, undated note]

Don't send any more reading matter as there is enough here to last us. And we were glad to get it. Joe sends "obliged to you" to Tom. Says it is the best chewing tobacco he has had since leaving home. He has not tried the other.

[On the back:, in J.W. McClurg's handwriting: Bowdle & Newcomb, Bank of Bowdle, Bowdle Edmunds Co, Dak. on "Insure in the New York Underwriters Agency" letterhead; motto: "Down the red lane are many thieves."]

Part Three

JOE MCCLURG, FANNIE'S BROTHER, *is the one person generally able to do the heavy lifting around the place, and he suffers from back problems from time to time. Fannie expresses some impatience, now and then, with Joe's slowness and peevishness, but it is hard to imagine how the project would have managed without him. Apparently not much labor was expected of the children—beyond housekeeping duties and their studies. Fannie, of course, is the indispensable entitity: the teacher, the manager, the cook, and the spiritual lodestar for the family. The erysipelas attack toward the end of October was a significant blow and had some effect no doubt on the decline in morale.*

Oct. 7

My Ever dear Charlie:

I only have a few minutes in which to write but I feel as if I must make use of the opportunity. Arthur is near me at work on examples. By the by we must send those problems with their answers. Of course we all set to work in good earnest to solve them, at first laughing at their simplicity. But after all they were somewhat puzzling. I need not tell you what mistakes were made and will leave you to guess those who solved them—if they are correct.

Joe is now at work at stable putting the house aside until good quarters for mules is established. We have had a real cold snap & a sprinkle of rain at the same time which makes us believe we ought to prepare for the worst. One coat of plaster is put on to the [illegible]—and part of that has second coat. Then we will have a general cleaning and the rest be done at once. It makes a great improvement in the house & when all is duly changed I will tell you how. The cupboard I am using but it is not quite done. Pa will go to Theodore this evening with [illegible] and some of the children. All pretty well. Children always say good night for you. All join me in much love to you. Kate has gone all day with one barefoot and one shoe on without stockings.

Fannie

October 10, 1886

This morning it is real cold and the sky all clouds. Pa and Mame were going to church about 7 miles from here in the Bacon neighborhood but we were afraid of the weather not knowing how it may terminate and they did not go. It is sufficiently cold to snow. We are all in the house now but Arthur & Jim who are having a frolic of some kind. Joe is drawing with Kate nearby and much interested. Emma is trotting around busy as a bee. Pa, Joe and Mary are reading. The latter talks a great deal about going home in the spring and I can't bear to tell her that I fear there is little hope. I know if her Aunt Emma's folks come up she can become reconciled. Of course it would be mighty nice if we could go back in the Spring, but not at all profitable. By the way George Terro is preparing to live on his place this Winter. But I think we need not fear any trouble; he is a young, harmless looking fellow and not large. He is trying to be very sociable but we will be as distant as possible under the circumstances. The old man was here a few nights ago looking for a cow and when we had not seen them he said he knew Herman (Kerchoff) had them but he would act the gentleman and not go on his place as he had given a promise to that effect.

The children came home from their ramble very tired, but I believe I did not tell you they took a lunch Friday and went to prairie dog town. They found a number of nice stones and had a good time. Yesterday Arthur found a large arrow head. I have a cute little one of red flint or something else that little Joe gave me. If you can have it set as a pin for yourself I will send it to you. It would make a nice little charm.

We are somewhat troubled now over our supply of water, it being small. Joe will take the cow home tomorrow but it would not pay to keep her and feed her any how. I intend speaking to Mr. J. and I think he can let us have a better cow —one that will supply us with butter. I churn at least twice a week and sometimes 3 times but the quantity is small.

We draw twice with the bucket to fill our bucket from the house, so it won't do to use that water for any thing else and it may hold out. Mr. Terro says the well we water from was 30 ft. deep with a big supply of water and we may have to dig that out as we can't depend on hauling in the Winter. If we do we will have it curbed. We may be able to have done in exchange of much work some way. Mr. J. will take mules this week and break sod. He is coming down this afternoon & will take letters to Theodore. On yesterday he thought he would. Can't you send me some insurance paper by mail? I'm out. Jim looks very anxiously for flipper rubbers that I believe you promised. I still have a $5 and 10 dol. draft & a little change. Pa paid the Hulls. Joe is not paid in full. I want to go to Bowdle soon and get shoes and some things—provisions included and you better send me a 25 dol. draft.

October 11, 1886

My Dearest Charlie:

My pen is bad, my ink is pale, but my love for you can never fail. Mr. J disappointed us yesterday so I will write a few lines more & Pa or A. will take them to The[odore] in the morning but they will not go until Wednesday. It has been trying to rain since yesterday and is pretty cold. Jodie and Mr. Johnson were dressed in full winter costumes today with the exception of caps and Jodie hadn't on his felt boots. The children are getting ready for bed although it is not 8 o'clock yet. Pa retires about 7 and Joe is having his smoke but will soon follow the children. Our stove does good service and our house is warm. We have supper about 5 o'clock and burn very little coal after that time and frequently not any, so don't be anxious about gas. Besides a little ventilation above windows I always open the door and we breathe pure fresh air you see.

[across top] 12. All well. Still cloudy. Pa & A. walk to Theodore.

I have been suffering a little from indigestion for a few days and do not feel very well. I guess I eat too much fruit—dried apples, for instance. I frequently fry them and they are first rate. I make ginger cookies sometimes as they can be made without eggs. And it is the only kind of cake I have made since leaving home. Joe took the cow home today and of course we will milk her but we will try and have another when we get a supply of water, which we are undecided about. If we had no mules we might manage without, and do without a cow; and save up water and only wash once a month, and bathe next 4 of July. Well we will manage some way and try and have it done cheaply if we can get help at all. Mr. Tanner has just dug his potatoes. The yield was not very large but beautiful and they had very little rain. If you could only stay with us next spring wouldn't we have a good time gardening. Tell Miss Mary we intend to beat her truck patch. If you can bargain for any good seed from her country friends I wish you would.

With heaps of love.

Fannie

Oct 13, 1886
Master James Draper, Theodore Dak

My Dear Jim:

I was greatly pleased yesterday to receive your nice letter and Mamma's. Although I was disappointed at the longitudinosity of hers I thought it was a mighty good letter for washday. I was proud to see what a nice letter you can write and proud also because Mamma said you were such a good hand that you had to do nearly all the churning. It is better to be the best butter maker than the poorest President. Ask Grandpa if it isn't. I feel sorry for the poor little gopher. Why dont you boys and Uncle Joe get that wolf into a hole and pour water on him? How big is he and does he look savage? Dont it make you boys afraid to go out hunting rocks when you know wolves are around? I just now passed two big brown bears by Hickman's shop that a man had brought to the fair. Aunt Sallie's children have a black puppy named Joe. It was not named after Grandpa like the rest of the children because it is a lady dog and is named Josephine for Mrs. Turner. It takes the cat up by the back with its teeth and runs nearly down to the stable. Sometimes the kitten's head is down and sometimes its tail. Joe thinks it is great fun and cat seems to like it.

Can you make as good butter as Mr. Johnson? or does Uncle Joe send over there for his buttah? Where did you get the Jack Rabbit Mamma said she was cooking? Did Arthur's gun pin fit all right? How do all of you like Dakota now? I hope Uncle Joe's plastering made the house look less like a barn. I think you and Joe and Mamma and Mame ought all to learn to ride the mules. Mamma must go over to see Mrs. Cookingham and some of the other neighbors and then she will feel better. I wish you children were here to gather nuts. Uncle Tom and Aunt Sallie are going to Linn Creek before long and they will get some hickory nuts. I am going to send your letter to Aunt Annie. Marshall has written me a letter wanting some stamps. Maybe I will send your letter to him. Have any of you boys written to Bird Dodd? He would like to hear from you. Our house is all right yet. How much water is in our well? Is there enough for house and mules and cow? How are Kate and Johnny? Does Johnny crawl any now? Hattie and Dick Carson have come over to the fair. If I go out I will write some of you what I see. Kiss all of them for me and tell Mamma I will write to her Sunday. Good bye. Your affectionate papa,

CC Draper

Oct 13, 1886

My Dear Fannie:

I have just answered Jim's letter and write you a line to say howdy. How I would love to see all of you—but that cant be now so you must take care of yourself and the rest so when I do you will be looking your

Dorie Draper's illustration of the Drapers' Walworth County homestead, ready for winter, 1886. This, of course, is the artist's best guess at the appearance of the homestead, derived from information in the letters. The only dimensions mentioned relate to the addition, which, Fannie guessed was about 9'x10'. The evidence for the shed roof, which, according to Welsch in Sod Walls, was rare, is from the sketch Charlie provided. (A settler quoted by David Laskin in his book The Children's Blizzard *called these "one way roofs.") Likely, we were generous in estimating 10'x24' as the interior dimension of the house.*

best. Dont work too hard. Mr. Greenleaf has been sick and I went down to see him the other night and he handed me to read Mame's letter to the family written when you first got up there. It had been passed around the neighborhood to be read and Mr. G. & family bragged on it so much that it made me right tickled. Mr. G. said I ought to be proud of that girl. I am. Bless her dear little heart. I am proud of her helping you with your work too. Fannie & Maggie are very anxious to get up to Dak & so is Sallie. If Tom could arrange it Sallie would be glad to go. Tom is doing quite well as a drummer but Sallie dont like the business. Your letters give me so much pleasure and I don't know how you find time to write such good ones. Let me know whether the various packages I send reach you. Hope the vests will be to your notion. Sallie thought they would fit. I got them at wholesale for $1.12½ each. Let me know anything I can get you here.

Of course Marshall has written you of the death of poor little Joe. It is very sad and I feel sorry for them. We have not heard how Jean is since. Hope all of you keep well. I think of you so much. You & the children are in my mind about the last thing before I go to sleep every night. Kiss all and give love to Gov. & Joe. Let me know whether I keep you supplied. All well here.

Affy yours
Charlie

Look out for weather and dont let anybody get caught in a blizzard. Never leave house far without lots of blankets. Blizzards come sometimes this time of year. I wish Mr. J. was through so he could be at home and let Tad take his place there.

Near Theodore Dak., Oct. 16, 1886

My Dearest Charlie:

Pa will start to Theodore in a few minutes and I will have to be in haste. I did want to write you a long letter but did not know he was thinking of going so early. If I were sure of having an opportunity to send tomorrow I would wait; but you know I depended on Mr. J. last Sunday and he did not come by. Now this wont go until Monday.

The boys are all off on a hunt this morning. It is cold but they are well wrapped and have gone to the gulches. There is nothing to shoot nearer here than little birds.

Your last letter containing a 10 dol. draft I received Monday. I have meant to acknowledge all you have sent and Pa says he has. I hope there is no mistake and none has been lost on the way. In my last I wrote for money expecting to go to Bowdle soon. We want to go next week if it is warm. 3 tons of coal will cost near $25. I now have $25 in drafts and with $1.25 Mrs. Hull owes me $7 besides. But we need not get all the coal just now as we could not bring it any way with other things. I may not be able to get the flannel I want but will only know by trying. The felt shoes I suppose will be a necessity. I have not had any cold feet with thin stockings and old shoes yet. But Joe complains a great deal of his feet, and Pa puts about every thing he can get hold of on his. Little Emma is still barefoot but never utters a complaint.

Our stove does first rate but does not come up to my old wood stove. It is too small to suit me after using a big stove so long. Emma is almost well and the rest of us are firstrate. Joe has renewed his plastering which means another mess—but comfort afterwards. As soon as we get things permanently arranged I will tell you just how every thing is. You know from the bunk back no plastering has been done & I guess Joe will begin that Monday. How I do want you with us. There will be no breaking done this fall. The backsetting will be attended to. I expect a letter from you this morning but often I do not get them until Monday. This is an unsatisfactory letter but I hope better than none. With oceans of love for your own dear self,

Fannie.

I hardly know what I have written but you will excuse any mistakes. Love to Robin and kindest regards to Mr. G. Give much love from all of us to all of our own dear ones whom we would very much love to see.

Do not expose yourself to Diphtheria. Hope none of the little folks will take it. Many thanks for Copy models. We hope to improve.

[c. 16 October, 1886]

Charlie: I am so afraid you might not approve of my letter to Marshall I thought I would enclose to you and if you approve just send it back and I can change date and send it on as there is plenty of time. Emma is crying for a pencil to "write to Papa." Joe McC killed a duck to day. Tad was down and I read a good letter from Em to him. The Tanner boys imbibe pretty freely some times and I hate so much for Jodie and Tad to go with them. When Joe left them in Bowdle he said Rupert was feeling his dram. Joe thinks that Jodie and Tad never drink any, but you know they might be induced to. I had a call today from Ada Tanner and Miss Miller, a neighbor of hers. We have had a few days of cold disagreeable trying to rain weather, and farmers will be delayed in putting in wheat.

Mr. Johnson wrote a mighty blue letter to Pa. If Wallace and Nixon are not liberal with him they are not white to say the least. They could easily afford to give him the farm if their hearts were big enough. Pa has written to Mr. J. to send out today.

16—Saturday. Joe will be off in a few minutes. A little better morning but cloudy. Arthur is out hunting. Children all well and rollicking. I am better this morning than I sometimes feel but have a slight neuralgia in one eye. Love and kisses from each one of us. Children enjoyed your letter. Kate has commanded another. Love to Sallie & others.

Affy,

Fannie

October 17, 1886

My Dear Fannie:

It is 2 ½ oclock Sunday and Tom and Sallie and the children are preparing to start out into the country but I concluded I would rather stay at home and write you. Their rig is a spring wagon & 2 little rabbit mules nearly the color of ours. I can remember just how our mules used to look coming over the hills from Theodore and I can imagine myself standing at the cabin door with you and the children watching first the mules' ears and then their heads and then the Governor in the wagon. I wish I was there now—and I hope the rest of you do too. Everybody has been to the fair this week except myself. When urged to go I reasoned thus: it will cost .10 out, .10 back, .25 to get in & .25 for extras. That will make .70 and I will nearly buy Johnny a pair of shoes and I don't want to go that badly. So I staid at house and worked and felt a great deal better than if I had gone and thought of all of you in that sod house practicing such strict economy, as I would have done. The only thing that I can think of that I have spent since returning to Lebanon outside of strict necessaries is .25 for Charleston and .10 for church. I made $1 one night at notary work and "invested" it in a Lottery ticket and much to my surprise drew a prize which will enable me to pay Annie & Mother the $32 I owe them for interest. Wasn't that nice? I got enough besides to pay for the material for the four flannel dresses for you and the little girls and make them. Wasn't that nice? Tom got him a new overcoat that he needed very badly and that was also nice. The tickets cost us $2 together and we drew $100 which we will get in a few days. We have been having big fun over it. It may not be very moral but it comes in right snug. I have been very sorry I could not pay that interest for I think they need it at home and you may imagine how tickled I was. Of course we are grieving that it wasn't $1000, but if we had got that we would have felt just as badly because it wasn't $10,000.

Jimmie was out at the fair 2 days. It was not as good as last year, but was pretty good. Frank took $10 prem. on Nola, $4.00 calf & $5.00 on apples, which he says Tad declares he is going to have. I will be glad when Tad is out on the cattle ranch. It keeps Frank wrought up all the time to see T. have so many privileges when he knows that he (Frank) does so much more work and is so much more deserving in every way. They would get along better without him than with him on the farm. But I must remember that we will do well if we manage our own children and not try to usurp the authority of other people. Impress all the time on our little fellows the hatefulness of selfishness. Guard them against "meum and tuum"—especially in our own family. One of the pleasantest things that I can think of separate from my brothers and sisters is the fact that money never produced the least hard feeling between any of us—nor as far as I can see is it ever likely to—the want of it might. And at the same time it is very gratifying to . . . [Remainder of the letter is missing.]

Oct. 22, 86

Dearest Charlie:

We did not go to Bowdle to day as was intended. We got up too late and the weather was rather threatening. Yesterday was a lovely day but it is cloudy and quite cold today. We may go tomorrow as our coal is almost out. Mr. Terro told Pa and Joe of a good place they could go to and get wood about 9 miles from here and they want to go some of these times. Mr. Terro and Lou are anxious to sell out by Spring and if we remain I hope they will succeed although they are very clever with us.

Our coal being low we have been burning some "chips" today. Sallie would have laughed could she have seen little Joe walk in as sober as a judge with a great heap of chips on the shovel that he could scarcely manage. I had to laugh although we have used quite a gooddeal so that it is getting common.

Joe moved the bunks out yesterday and we all slept on the floor last night. Emma and I took our same corner as when you were here. Joe expected to finish entirely today but I hardly think he will. When done it will finish up the plastering and you must rejoice with me for it will be a relief. Then I can arrange things and keep half way decent. I shall put my curtains also and put on the letter D.

I would greatly rejoice if Tom could arrange some way to have Sallie up here and all others that want to come but I believe they will want to get away much worse than they ever wanted to come—don't you? If you could be with us of course I could so happy any where I know. But this separation is hard. I would have sent a postal card to Theodore yesterday but thought we would get off today.

These printed words were done entirely by Kate. She can spell mighty well. You can see that Joe was independent of help. Jim will ask how to spell a word sometimes. Pa and Arthur took mules over to Mrs. Terros for water this evening—for the mules. I love to take a game of checkers with you and the little folks. I so often think of their little cunning faces and cute ways and would love dearly to see them. Is there no prospect of selling to Ch. Smith. It would be splendid to live in our home again. I am afraid too good to be true. All join in heaps of love to one and all.

Affy

Your wife,

Fannie D.

Not q. 6 o'clock. We start to B. in a few m. Be sure and give my
love to Miss Mary for I think a greatdeal of her. Remember me to Mr.
G. and folks and Mrs. W.J. Beautiful day-

Oct. 24, 1886

My Dearest Fannie:

Your weekly letter came yesterday instead of Monday or Tuesday as
usual, and was a pleasant surprise. You don't know how much pleasure
your letters give me—telling as they do all about our little home matters.
That is the best kind of news I can have. I imagined the boys off in the
gulches hunting north of swan creek and as they went up a grassy ravine
a big black wolf sat up in the way and showed his teeth and then Arthur
put in a buck shot shell and got the little boys behind him and laid the
old wolf out and had material for letters to all of the boys in Lebanon. It
would be a big card for him if he could have killed a wolf on his birthday. Did you remember it last Monday? I wish I could have sent him a
present—hope some of you gave him one. Give him 14 kisses for me and
tell him to kill 14 Jack Rabbits. You have not told me about any game
yet though you mentioned once the fact that you had rabbit for dinner.
I suppose he came and gave himself up without catching. I am awfully
sorry about that well. If you do conclude it best to dig a stock well I
would not go to much expense to wall it with wen[sic] if wooden curb-
ing was cheaper. Hull can figure on that. I believe water could be gotten
quickly down the ravine toward Theodore where Joe and I saw a moist

place. He and the Governor will know where I mean. It is too bad that after all of our work and worry and expense that the well does not furnish sufficient water. As you did not mention it in your last letter I take it for granted that you still have enough for house purposes. But is it likely to hold out for that during the winter? What does the Governor think about it? I will look with interest for your description of the internal arrangements of the house when Joe gets plastering done. Tell Joe I want to learn all the particulars about that and about how he fixed the stable. Also I want to know all about that other room to the house and how it works and how you like it etc etc. How many loads of clay did it take and how did the mortar work and did it make a nice looking job and how many coats did you have to put on and did it dry out without giving any of you bad colds? There are questions enough. How does the Governor occupy his time and how many blankets does he sleep under now? Eight in August ought to mean 18 in December. Does he sleep in the house or still stick to the tent? Has he been hunting yet with Arthur's gun? He said he was going to. It seems to me that Theodore is a long walk for him. Have they ever ridden one of the mules off without the other? How are you all getting along generally and do you take a walk every day? Tell Mame I thought so much of that little stone she sent me that I sent it to Mermod Jaccards & Co. to see if it had any value and also to know how much it will cost to grind it into a set. I hope I will hear from them before I close this letter so will write what they say. In the meantime have the little fellows save all of the chat stones they find and if they are not of any value sometime they will be very interesting to us and to give away to our friends after we all get to living in our old house again. Yes I would like the best kind to have that little arrow head and I will see if I cant have it set into a scarf pin or something of the kind. Tom went to Sunday School with the girls today and came home insulted because Fannie laughed at him for getting out his assafetida bag to play with. Sallie makes them all wear them and on big Tom refusing she pinned one to the caudal appendage of his shirt after he went to sleep. He kept smelling it all day but did not know where it was till next night. I dont presume it is very efficacious without faith—but he has not taken diphtheria anyhow. The scare is over and school going again. They say Ruby is conducting a very good school. I see the children's little friends, too numerous to mention, and they are always interested in knowing all about them I hear Flossie had a letter from Mame. Does Arthur write to the Herndon boys?[1] I was over to the farm the other night and staid awhile. Charley has got to walking and talking in his sleep. The other night he was talking to Arthur at a great rate but I dont suppose Arthur heard him. Jim wrote me a real nice letter and I wish the others would. Tell the Governor I will write him. Of course Marshall wrote about the death of poor little Joe. Jean seems to be doing well. Annie writes that Mother and Fannie and Arthur have gone to housekeeping in Arthur's house for the winter and Fannie is working with Arthur at $10 a week. Would that be nice for the boys? By the way dont say anything to home folks about that interest for I could not send it after all. Had other pressing uses for the money. Will pay in the winter if possible. Annie and Laura[2] seem to be busy and I hope are doing well. Annie writes about some school [illegible] the children but I left her letter at the office and will have to consult it. We are all well here. We will likely walk over to the farm this afternoon and get some persimmons. Jim goes to Richland[3] tomorrow. He had a busy day yesterday & hopes

---

1 Old friends of the family.

2 Charlie's oldest sister.

3 A town just east of Lebanon.

to do well down the road. I sent the children some books yesterday and think there are some pictures in them to paint. This week I had to get myself some clothing—sox, undershirts and boots. I got the latter heavy enough for Dakota in February so if I can go up then or anytime while the weather is cold they will be comfortable. I hope the Gov. finds his flannel shirts comfortable and that they fit and also you do your vests. Sallie is working on your dress and as soon as done I will forward it by mail, or if cheaper by express. She has Charley with her so has to do more of her own house work. Let us know about money & cow etc etc. Tell M. J.[4] I will see Clough about hay bales. I had over-looked it. Kiss all of the little fellows for me and give them lots of love from papa. Do you get enough sleep now? What kind of hours do you keep? I wish I could do something to make it easier and more pleasant for you. I would so love to see all of you. Tell Joe & Kate I wish they would send me two gopher skins for my ears this winter. The stone Kate gave me with a red center is beautiful if I can only get it finished, and I think Mame's will be equally so. Ask Joe to find me a nice one. Robin has got home from Kansas and reports Oscar and family well and nicely situated.

Goodbye & love & kisses to all.

Affy,

Charlie

The weather reports show it freezing with you. I hope you wont suffer. Wish you were here and I could stand the weather there for you. My contest will soon come off. Send [illegible] it attention.

---

4 Marshall Johnson

Theodore Dak. Oct. 25, '86

My Ever Dear Husband:

You see I have made my Bowdle trip and instead of a fat pig I brought home a side of bacon and a sack of beans. I will enclose the bills so you see prices etc. It took a lot of money but all seemed necessary for health excepting calico which is for curtains and my cupboard, but that was not a big extravagance. There is gum and candy that could have been dispensed with, but living as we do you will appreciate that part of it. I really only ordered 10 cts. of candy and 15 cts. of apples but the rascal left the apples out—I presume by mistake and it was a great disappointment to me when I discovered the mistake on the way home. He gave us three beautiful large apples as we were leaving and I gave one to Jim and brought one to Kate. The other was Pa's and he had it divided between the other three giving each a nice large piece. Kate shared hers with Emma. The former was asleep when we got home but rose very early next morning to get her wax—and she says "it looks just like old Santa Clause has been here." Then I told her to look on the middle of the table and she would find something for herself. She was terrible tickled (I have just put Emma down.) tickled when she saw the big apple and soon went to work on it. The children all thought I had been mighty good to remember them with so "many good things." Little Emma eats the crackers principally and loves them. When we had the cow the children (in fact all) enjoyed rice. We have hardly decided about a well yet but will either have to haul from Terro's (and it would freeze this winter) or take mules over there every day (we water from there now—mules) and there will probably be days that will be too cold for that. Joe says he can go down about 10 ft. himself and then it would necessitate help after that. Mr. Terro told Pa that he would dig that old well out for 4 or 5 dols. and it could be covered over with straw in such a way to protect it this winter and nothing more done to it until spring. He says the water is splendid and soft, and in abundance. It is probably the best thing to do as the water seems to be insured.

> To market to market
> To buy a fat pig
> Home again home again
> Jiggity Jig

Oct. 27

I shall go back to my Bowdle trip. Jim & I were pretty cold for 2 hours until we reached Peckham's and warmed nicely and then I got back on a box by Jim and by the aid of a double blanket & Father's shawl (we were already dressed with warm clothing & wraps) we kept warm. It was about 8 o'clock when we reached home but the wagon cover was down between us & Pa & Mr. Terro (whom we had to take) and we did not suffer the least & Jim went to sleep lying partly in my lap. No telling when we would have gotten home if Mr. Terro hadn't been along. So far he is a good neighbor. His wife has never been here & probably will not come.

Mame got along nicely with little Emma and says she was not at all troublesome and she would give her rice when she asked for T and would run and play until hungry again. She is the sweetest cutest baby and has a great many words and is learning to talk so fast & seems to understand everything. I think her eye teeth are through.

Don't you think Bowdle prices compare pretty well with those of

Lebanon. Maybe a little high. The stockings were the heaviest factory made I ever saw (for Mamie). The flannel is a good piece of plaid. Calico good. I did not get a supply of fruit as I could not find country dried and the other is too high. We will try again. Our supply of flour is still not gotten and a few other things. We only got about 500 lbs. of coal. Only send money as you can make it most convenient for we can manage to get flour from Theodore very nicely any time and we have a fair supply of other things as you see from bills. And coal will last quite awhile. I am sorry you have to send so much. I am so afraid sometimes we will never come out ahead but hope you don't worry about it. If we can only get well and keep well, I think other matters we cannot help ought not to be a source of trouble, continually. I was very much pleased with Mr. & Mrs. Wilson those we traded with mostly. Mrs. Echuo called a day or two since & I was very much pleased with her. My face was then swelling badly and she so kindly offered to return and do any thing she could for me in the way of washing or any thing. We have no water here and then I have not been able to wash for a couple of weeks. Not feeling right well you know. Probably it was my face disease in the system.

I hardly know what to say to you about my face. I don't want to frighten you but it is the most terrible looking face I ever saw. Probably the swelling has ceased, and my eye is almost closed and the swelling is above it but not in the forehead. There is scarcely any soreness now even by pressure. At the beginning the glands back of my chin and the jaw bones were very sore. The part just below the eye and nearest the nose looks almost like a raw piece of beef. And a part of the surface is rough and some caked near the skin only, as well as I can tell. Right below the eye is greatly puffed & soft. I rather believe it has run its course and will soon show indications of breaking away in some form. It looks now as if it could never look like my face any more but yet I expect it to and hope and trust it will. It shows no sign of coming to any head. It would be a bad place for a scar wouldn't it? It would just spoil my beauty and then what would you do?[5]

The children are all out "rock picking" as Kate calls it. Jim remained back here to take care of Emma but he has been gone with her quite a while. Joe is finishing up the store room roof with sod. Yesterday he & Pa assisted Mr. J. in breaking sold for him and themselves also—as they want to put up a house as soon as it is convenient now as Joe has secured a claim. Mr. J. is too busy to visit us. Jodie will come by this evening on his way to the office. I must get your letter to night. You don't know how I love you old dearest. Why are we separated? I hear the children. Big love to all—

Fannie

Oct. 28, 1886

Dear Charlie:

I am better this morning and the swelled face is considerably smaller if not handsomer.

Rest are well.

Boys all out at play—also Kate. Emma trotting around in mischief.

Mame singing and rocking, waiting on me to assist in dish washing. Pa getting ready to take draft to Mr. J. They will be so gratified as they have been requesting something. Received yours of 17 & 19 last

---

5 Fannie had erysipelas, an acute bacterial infection.

night containing drafts. Joe building little house near ravine not a great way from house. Pa ready,

Affy,

Fannie

Night of 29.

Mr. J. & J. will go to Bowdle tomorrow. Still improving. Love to one and all

Night—Didn't go today—Still improving. feel much better. Weather fine.

Papa last night to stray cats come hear. We boys thought they were awful nice. Uncle Joe took out the bunks and some of the other things to day and plastered. Mrs. Rosett gave us a black and white kitty her name is Lolly.

Your sun Joe [age seven]

Marks representing Emma's writing [age 17 months]

Dear Papa

I send you a stamp will you please get me two boxes of caps for my pistol.

Jim [age ten]

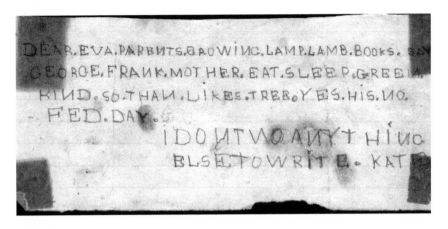

Dear Eva parents growing. Lamp. Lamb. Books. Say. George. Frank. Mother. Eat. Sleep. Green. Kind. So. Than. Likes. Tree. Yes. His. No. Fed. Day.
I dont no any thing else to write. Kate [age four]

Walworth Co, Dakota, Wednesday 12 [noon?] 27 Oct 1886
CC Draper

Dear Friend,

After saying all are well, except that Fannie has a slight attack of Erysipiles in the face (one cheek), but which has spent its force, I will mention the business that calls for this. The tree contest, comes to trial at 10 a.m. Saturday 13 Nov. at Land Office at Aberdeen. It will be necessary for you to send a draft for expenses of traveling etc. for Joe and two witnesses. I may go as one witness, getting Jodie to sleep here the night we may be gone. It might be two nights. Terow will go as one witness, charging nothing but expenses. We will take R.R. at Bowdle, leaving mules there, and think we may get back to Bowdle night of 13th, starting from here morning of Friday, the 12th. I calculate that the necessary expenses will amount o $22 or over, saying nothing about costs of trial at Aberdeen and amt. (if any) to pay Carter. As to that you know as much as I do. You will have no time to lose for the draft to get here. U.S. mails move slowly as yet out here. If it does not get here in time we must draw on you. I think I had better go along in order to save time, being more accustomed to such things. The trial should not consume more than 15 minutes. Everything is in good shape and no defense can be made. You had better send a draft for $25 or more. It will not be wasted. Fannie will write you to go off with this and give family news (if she have any). The children now all off on the rocky points toward Terow's, except Jim and Emma (I'm being nurse to-day). Emma is just going to sleep. Fannie is cooking beans—my choice, you know. Joe is finishing roof (sodding) on new room. This p.m. he hauls sod for a very important building—not a large one, however. On night of 25th the mules first occupied the stable. That now is their home at night, with all the hay they will eat. Mr. J. and Jodie are well and building stable and preparing for sod-house. Joe and I are also preparing. This is a fine day—wind from the South and it is pleasantly cool.

Love to all.

Truly & Affly

JW McClurg

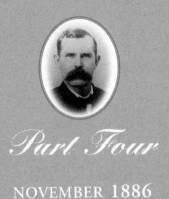

Part Four

THE LITTLE DETAILS, THE SIMPLE *activities of daily living, the snapshots of the immediate scenes in the soddy continue to dominate in the November letters. Business is clicking along—preparations for winter, for Thanksgiving; thoughts about Christmas are emerging. The house is remarkably comfortable, and there are indications of reaching out to neighbors for society. Lonesomeness is developing ("Why ain't you here tonight?" Fannie wonders). There are recurring mentions of returning to Missouri in the spring, with the children chiming in about it; problems with water; and blizzards toward the end of the month—powerful themes emerging in the letters.*

Theodore, Dak. Nov 1, 86

My Dearest Charlie:

I feel kind of lonesome like and will start a letter to you. The children have just returned from a ramble. Have been playing horse over the prairie—said it was too cold to hunt stones. All were gone but Emma and she was around looking up mischief. Upset some cracklings a little while ago and then helped herself. I must take her now. The little tad has nursed and gone again. Boys and Kate out having a loud play of some kind. Mame is opening a can of tomatoes for dinner (we have two meals) Pa is out on the prairie looking at some claim. He loves to go and he loves to walk. He took A's gun today for the first time and I do hope he will kill something for I know it would please him. Joe is hauling sod to finish out house. Mr. J. & Jodie went to B. Saturday but did not return until yesterday. I sent by them for fresh meat to get according to price, and do you think beef was 15 cts. per lb. And they only offered Mr. J. 2 ½ cts on foot. They only got me 3 lbs; but we had a splendid mess for breakfast, and didn't we enjoy it though? And I am serving the remainder for dinner. We also bought 2 hogs a few days ago at 3 cts. To be killed Wednesday. They came to $9.00 There are not many in the country and we thought it was best to secure while we had a chance although they are not large and will not produce a greatdeal of lard, but they are mighty nice as Mr. Tero killed one of the same lot and let us have 20 lbs to be returned when ours are killed. Fresh meat is *awful* good—ain't it? You ought to see us all eat. Arthur remarked at table this morning, that he would be ashamed to eat in Lebanon at any one's table but his Aunt Emma's. Kate is a hearty fat little toad and does not grow any handsomer, but is a bright happy little soul. Mamie is maturing faster than I want her to. But girls will all have to be women sooner or later I suppose—if they live, and of course she cant be an exception. Bless her heart she is a great comfort. It is now night and I have just gotten the baby down and am doing my best to get others to follow suit. Pa has already gone and poor Joe is nursing a sore tooth which he fears will trouble him all night. The other children are beginning to make preparations for bed—but against their will—as they want to paint and draw and all have been around the table having a big time with their pictures. They were so delighted with those little books you sent them and have already gotten loads of pleasure out of them. They commenced their studies again today—having lost all of last week on account of my sickness. It is so hard to have them study regularly but they will learn something this Winter I hope and I think they are having a little experience that will never be lost on them but always prove a benefit. I must congratulate you on your 50 dol. prize which pleased me very greatly although I do not approve of gambling but I like to have you in luck when you take a chance. Don't invest too much next time. And don't let Tom be carried away. If it had only been 10000 though! Would we soon have gotten out of these diggings? Well it was mighty nice and gave you some help any how.

At B. they charged me 15cts. for cashing 3 drafts. At one place where I traded best the merchant willingly cashed it. Some time ago you wanted to know what new stove vessels I got and I believe I could never think to tell you. A steamer & stove pot were all that I got extra. Pa tried to get a bill of items from them and did not succeed so it was never satisfactory to me. I tried the coal oil recipe but it lessened the labor very little for me. I may have misunderstood directions as they were not explicit. Pa understood it just as I did. The cars are running regularly to B & you can send by Express but I don't know as to terms. It might be cheaper to send book and medicine by mail. I am so afraid I wont know how to use them after I get them but I will do some big thinking if necessary. Will Mother return in this month? Children are beginning to talk Christmas. My erysipelas eye is still very weak and my face is not quite well yet. Good night old dearest. Why aint you here to night?

Heaps of love to all of our dear ones—affy—Fannie.

Nov. 2—1886

We had a glorious rain—it having rained most all night. Of course it has given water for awhile. The children say the old well is about ½ full. I must do a little washing to day on the strength of it, but I am not able to wash many pieces. Joe & Pa will go to Theodore pretty soon and cast their first votes for the Territory. I presume Mr. J. and Jodie will also go. The Democrats are making a hard fight or have been. I hope it will avail nothing.

I expect a letter from you to day. I do love dearly to get your letters.

You poor old fellow! You ought not to confine yourself so closely but go out more, and spend a *nickle* once in a while any how. In earnest Charlie—you are having too severe a time and it makes me feel badly to think of it. I would spend something on myself when I felt like it. You ought to have gone to the Fair. I do wish you were here and we would have a good time *all the time.*

Pa says send the book by mail. It will cost no more and probably not as much and will be brought right to Theodore.

The children all talk of going home in the Spring—but occasionally their Grandpa puts a damper on their feelings and it gives Mame the blues until I give her another talk. If it is but for us to stay—she will be more reconciled when Fannie & Maggie come up here. But now she wont own to it. All ready to start—

Affy—Fannie Draper

Dorie Draper's illustration depicts what the homestead may have looked like after the first blizzard. The outhouse apparently never got finished, although Fannie says—without providing details—that they got by just fine. The stable was apparently quite comfortable, but the well froze and the mules had to be taken to a neighbor for watering.

Theodore Dak. Nov. 3/86

My Dearest Charlie:

As I had a hundred and one questions to answer I thought I would take time by the forelock and begin now. Your good & interesting letter of 24 I received yesterday and will now proceed with my answers. No we never have any game for there seems to be none nearer than the gulches and I am afraid our son Arthur is too lazy to go so far with his gun. He would go twice that distance to hunt for stones. Joe & Pa will go for wood tomorrow and intend taking the gun and in all probability they will get grouse or a jackrabbit. The one or part of a one that I was cooking on wash day was given to us by Jodie. He frequently kills game of some kind—seems to be fortunate in coming across it. Don't worry about supply of water—Amongst us we will manage it cheaply. Joe said to night in all probability he could swap work with Mr. Terro. By the way Mrs. T sent word by Pa to day that she was coming to see me some of these times. She sent me some very nice butter. They killed our hogs over there to day and the old man helped them part of the day but wouldn't charge anything. So far, we wouldn't want a better neighbor so far as accommodation goes.

Our plastering looks well for a rickety sod house and is a very great improvement over what you saw and so much cleaner. It is dark of course and cracked all over but sticks splendidly and I am right proud of it— yet I don't know how it compares with that of others. It took scarcely a wagon load without sideboards on. It dried so fast that it would give no one time to take cold from it. Joe may get time to plaster other room and it will make it so much nicer about keeping things clean. I am afraid he won't get time as his own house is to be built yet and there are still other things to be done here. Out house not half done—hay to be hauled— wood and coal to be gotten and other little things fixed up. Maybe hen house made. All are in bed now. I have been a long time getting Emma to sleep and have just put her down. Pa says he only spends about 12 hours in bed now. I am always the last to bed, generally go about 9 o'clock. Not often before. When I get well and my eye is strong again I want to sew some at nights. I am doing no sewing now but mending. Our fire is out and I am chilly—Good night dearest. Wish I was with you or you up here. Hope some other arrangement can [be]made in the Spring. Good night!

Thursday about 2 o'clock. It is bright and cool and the wind is blowing most terribly. The children have gotten up quite an excitement over what they think is a prairie fire as they smell the smoke very strongly. There may be one somewhere in the distance. Arthur has been digging around the tent. You look out most any where and see a tumbling and whirling at breakneck speed. Did you see any before you left here? They are almost round in appearance and travel very fast in a wind.[1] Pa and Joe started out early for wood this morning and I am afraid they will have an unpleasant day. I wanted to render lard but Joe couldn't cut up the hogs. I have done a little washing this morning in about a handful of water. I haven't had enough water for sometime to do a decent washing. I am also trying to make a little liverwort [sic] but have no sage for it. We had liver and melt for breakfast and thought it mighty good. I must get dinner now. What books did Annie mean? Have you written anything to her about studies for Arthur and Mame? I have wanted to but delayed from different reasons. I am now at one end of the table waiting on some of the children to get through with dinner, having finished mine. I had real nice liverwort for dinner and wished for you. I had no sage but flavored with an onion.

Nov. 4–1886

It is now night and all are around the table but Arthur, and he is preparing kindling for his Uncle Joe in his absence. Did it of his own accord. It is near 6 o'c and Joe has just announced his Grandpa & Uncle Joe and I am relieved.

They have had their suppers and Pa has just told us good night and Joe is undressing. Pa came in ahead of Joe to night and brought a beautiful big jackrabbit killed by the latter. Joe had gotten out and was walking and came in soon after with a nice large grouse. So we will have game for dinner tomorrow. Wish you could come over and eat with us. I saw

---

1 Fannie likely refers to tumbleweed.

nice large cranberries in Bowdle. Arthur is the only one up now and he is reading Young American Speaker. Arthur is a first rate boy and improving all the time. Is so good now to help me. Of his own accord he commenced reading his bible through on his 14 anniversary. I gave him a lead pencil on the 19 as I had no opportunity to get it the 18. But he was very much pleased as it was something he needed and wanted. And Mame came across a little candy that she gave him but he kept only a bite of that. When you write do not refer to what I have said about Arthur for I am afraid Pa & Joe think all of the boys bad. But it does not matter particularly for they are pretty good boys if they do kill little birds and play on the hay sometimes. The latter they will not do any more though. Our store room is not larger than 9 x 10 inside. I do not know exact size. I want to rearrange every thing in there tomorrow and take provision box out of here in then, if Joe can only give me a little help. I believe he does the best he can but he is *so slow* I almost get out of patience. But I dont let him know how I feel. I do so much want him to help me in here with some things that I can't do, and it does seem as if he will not get ready before Spring. That room has a window in the east—only one sash, and the door faces the south. *This* room is very comfortable, *that* adding to the warmth of course. I believe a sod house is warmer than a brick and we don't begin to feel the wind in here. Coal oil is out. Good night.

Nov. 6

I haven't had a chance to write any more until now and I must finish as Pa wants to go to office this afternoon and I suppose this will be my last opportunity to send until Tuesday, then he will want to go for Monday's mail. It is now 1 o'c and I am sitting down to rest for the

first time. We are having pretty cold weather but don't know how thermometer stands. Our house is warm and comfortable. Don't be uneasy
about blizzards. We will run no risks. Children play out most of the
time but generally well wrapped. Our dresses came yesterday. They are
quite pretty and fit well. Many thanks to Sallie and you. I hope little
Mary is well and also all others. How I would love to see all the folks,
little and big. I so often think of how Sallie's little ones used to come
in, and how sweet and nice they always were and so afraid of giving me
trouble—bless their hearts, I do want to see them. Is Tom as nice as
ever? I will keep leaving your question. Jodie took Alie one night and
each behaved well but of course they are very much attached. Alie is
also a good riding mule and very gentle. I do not take a walk every day,
but will try to for your sake. Pa still keeps in the tent. You refer to
Christmas what I have been wanting to speak of. I have been intending to see what could be gotten in Bowdle but will have to leave that
with Pa as I suppose I should hardly make another trip. Kate must have
a doll—also Emma but a very cheap one will do her & Kate's only a
little better. Mame would rather have a book than any thing else. I
never saw any one so fond of reading in my life. Arthur is nearly her
equal. I believe Jim and Joe would rather have knives than any one
thing and Pa can get those. We can get candy in Bowdle I suppose as
cheaply as in Lebanon. What a splendid time we could have on nothing if you were here. I have written so much and said so little but I
must end it. Loads of love to the dear ones & yourself

Nell is sending Mame the St. Nicholas.

Do you know anything about our clock key? If you have it, send
it on.

I wish you could see Emma. We think she is smart and mighty
cute. She says almost any word she wants to now. Has all of her teeth but

two and I believe they show under the skin. Kate has just said, "Mama, I think it is cold enough to freeze somebody."

FMD

Nov. 4, 1886

My dear Fannie:

Today your two letters came with your postal card all same mail and you may know how distressed I am to learn of your sickness. I at once wrote [illegible] quoting all you said about it and symptoms and added what struck me about the appearances in August when you were sick and told her to get Dr. Dryor to put up some medicine to send you by mail for you to take if he thought you able after this spell wore off—if it didn't get there in time to do any good now—and also a supply so you could have it in case you should be attacked again. I also wrote her to ask him if the book and family supply of medicine could be sent by mail and if not I will have him order it sent by Express to Bowdle when I hear from him. I hope you will get the medicine promptly for yourself and truly hope you will have gotten over the attack by this time. You ought not to try to wash when not feeling right well. I would get Mrs. Kerchoff to do it. For you to get sick makes me feel like it was a bad thing for us to undertake the move up there. I hope it will not prove so. As I cannot tell whether you have received all the drafts to make sure I send you $50 in this. I think you rec'd $25 after returning from Bowdle. I have since sent the Gov. $15 knowing the trip to Aberdeen would have to be made. I paid Mr. Carter $20 so I suppose there will be no expense except fare to there and back. Note was to cover $5.00 of it at Land Office. $5.00 advertising and 10 fee for [illegible]. If contest is successful I suppose [illegible] be necessary to make the filing in [illegible] my name and 5 acres can be broken [illegible] Spring. I have had all the children's letters delivered—all eight to Roy. They are all [illegible] get them but Jim was disappointed that there was none for him. I also read a [illegible] to Frank. Tad says he will start to Dakota next Monday. That was the first I knew of his going, but I think it is a good move for Mr. J. & Tad too. They are all well. Little Mary is about well again but weak. Jim is at work on teeth—has 2 sets under way on 1 impression besides. Will have to make some of Hart's over. Tuesday was election day. I will write you about it Sunday. The Republicans were successful beyond their most sanguine expectations. Gov's letter recd with yours. Am so sorry about water. How do you like your storm door. Lay in a good supply of coal and provisions now. I havent yet had time to look over the bills you sent but will do so. Love & kisses to the little fellows and your dear self. Will look anxiously for your next letter. Love to all.

Affectionately yours

CC Draper

Suppose dresses are all there by this time.

Theodore Dak. Nov. 10/86

My Dearest Charlie:

It is now 7 o'clock and Pa says it is bed time but I will write some for fear I wont have time tomorrow and as Pa and Joe will leave for Bowdle Friday I want to send this letter by them. I have just gotten the 4 younger ones to bed. Arthur is writing to Bird Dodd. (I wish you could see the last letter A. wrote to the Herndon boys, he is improving in his writing.) Mame is reading the Globe Democrat for want of something better. Pa and Joe are sitting near by and as quiet as church mice. Pa and Joe went after wood today about 5 miles and the latter killed 3 grouse and just after he returned he saw one right near our stable and got the gun quickly and killed it. So we have two nice meals of chicken ahead of us and plenty of good pork. Jim and Arthur walked to Theodore today after the mail. The little tads wanted to go and of course it takes several hours but they didn't seem to mind it. They brought me a nice letter from you and now it will be a whole week before I can get your last Sunday letter—but they are so nice when they do come. Kate, Jim, and [word omitted] were delighted with their letters. It tickled Kate terribly. That little thing deserves almost the sole credit for what she has learned. I don't think I have heard her recite exceeding ½ doz. times. She would ask any of us what a certain picture was and how to spell it. And I would say now Kate look at the letters while you spell so you will learn them and would have her to spell slowly—and I noticed that she was always particular to look closely at her words. She is very persistent and now there is not a big letter any where that she doesn't know, and she knows most of the small ones. She learns to spell very quickly. Her Grandpa thinks she learns rapidly—but Emma is his girl and she loves her Grandpa too. I am so sorry little Mary is sick and do hope it will prove to be nothing serious.

Joe and Pa also went for wood yesterday but as a blizzard seemed to be brewing they hastily got a small load and returned. The wind was from the N.W. yesterday and it was very cold with a slight mist part of the time but we were about out of fuel and they felt compelled to go. This is a beautiful day, but bright and cold. It has been freezing all day— still Emma runs out barefoot every chance she gets. She is getting fat. The little flannel dresses came a few days ago and are mighty nice fits and real pretty. They are proud of them but more especially Kate, and she wore hers Sunday. I will wait for Winter before I put them on for good. Also Mame's and mine. Mame wore hers Sunday. I wish now that I had gotten Sallie to make Arthur's and Kate's flannel under clothing but I have gotten the flannel and will commence them soon. I have been mending for Pa and Joe to day. I think Pa and Joe ought to have flannel drawers. The latter has good knit shirts and there is a package of some kind at Theodore for Pa from Marshall and Arthur said paper was torn and it looked like red flannel. I presume they are shirts. We will know tomorrow. He has some old linsey drawers he thinks I can fix up, but I doubt it. I do the biggest patching on his socks that I ever did "in all my born days." Arthur couldn't bring package because it was registered. If Sallie should want to send Pa anything for Christmas, send a ther-mometer as he thinks we ought to have one but I wont spend money for one. He has not asked it at all but I know how he feels. I believe if S. would make them I would get flannel for their drawers and send them by mail. I will try to write more tomorrow night.

Nov. 11, 1886

Dear Papa,

I was so glad to get your letter yesterday. Arthur got a letter from Bird Dodd and he said he saw you and you said we was going home in the spring and I tell you it tickled us the prairie dog was awful good, but Grandpa would not try it. Grandpa went to theodore to day and I got a letter from Roy. Grandpa was so glad that Laclede Co. went republican that he threw his old hat so high it came down on the house. I got the flipper rubber, and I was so glad. ask tom if he shoots a flipper now. Give my love to all

Your affectionate son Jim

Kate sends these dolls to Tom [In Fannie's handwriting across the bottom.]

Nov. 11

Dear Papa yesterday uncle Joe killed four grouse. One down to the barn. Uncle Joe and Grandpa hauled wood three times. The old well has froze tight. Arthur and I got on the edge of it. I am in the second reader our kitty jumps up to the latch and rattles it like a person when she wants to get in. Emma got this letter down on the floor and got it dirty. I don't fill like writing any more next time I will try to write a loger [sic] letter. Good bye

Your son Joe

Nov. 11, 1886

Dear Charlie:

It is again night—my time for writing as I am too busy during the day generally and then I have so many more interruptions—although the children are all around the table and Emma is giving trouble. I shall have to get her to sleep pretty soon and then I may be able to write with satisfaction. I can scarcely write now. I received your letter of 4 today and on learning your distress felt so sorry I had written you of my sickness—as I am well now. I don't think I should have written you about it if I had known it was really erysipelas; but I did not know how it might terminate (as my face looked so terribly) and thought I ought to let you know. I received $50.00 in drafts to day. Pa received the $15 a few days ago. I still have the $25.00 so don't be in a hurry to send more—we are getting along finely now and Pa will add to our supplies on this trip and bring home some coal. The mules are doing pretty well on hay. Alie looking better than Pete as he always has. We are now giving a little bran and wheat to Pete especially as he seemed to need something more and has a most outrageous appetite. They are so good and kind that we are all attached to them. About that nice farm and house up here—none of the children will listen to. They all looked doleful indeed when I read it aloud. They cant bear the idea of staying here longer than Spring and are always planning for their trip home and what big times they will have when they get there. Mame often speaks of how she will fix up her little blue room again and gets a world of pleasure out of it. I always let her talk and frequently make suggestions feeling at the same time that she may be sadly disappointed. Their little correspondents all tell them that you say you intend to bring them home in the Spring and they are counting on nothing else. Of course you know I would be more than delighted but I can hardly hope for any thing so good, for I cannot see how you can manage it with advantage to ourselves and you have already made so many sacrifices. But wouldn't it be too good almost if we could go back or you come here? Can there be found a good way? Pa got the package from Marshall today and it contained 2 under shirts of flannel—2 pr sox and a pr. of fulled mittens—all good. He talked as if he would send another package before long thinking he could buy more cheaply there. I don't know what Pa will write him. You please have the drawers made for them—2 prs. Each, and they will not buy now. M. wrote Pa that he heard through you that he was greatly in need of clothing and he expressed much regret on not knowing sooner and wanted Pa to let him know here after—as if he would. If he would send a little money once in a while Pa would not spend it in riotous living. Don't speak of this.

I am glad little Mary is up again. I will write again about Christmas things but have preparations to make for an early breakfast now. Pa wants to be off by 7 a.m. Bless your dear good self. I feel sometimes as if I must go to you in spite of everything. You don't know how I want to see you, and I feel now when I get another glimpse of you I will never let you go. I hope you are well of your cold. Do take care of your self. Is your hearing any worse?

Send me a roll of insurance paper as I don't want to spend money for any. I dream some horrible things about you sometimes. What are you doing?

Theodore Nov. 13, 1886

My Dearest Charlie:

Supper is over and although all of the little ones are still out of bed and as noisy as usual I must begin a letter any how. This is the second night we have been alone but those I would fear at all are away from home and I hardly think I need fear anything from them, as they are our best friends so far. George Terro is in Minn. with a sick bro. and Mr & Ms. Terro went to Bowdle—also to Aberdeen with Pa (the former as a witness for Joe), and will return when they do. They took 4.00 lbs. of butter in our wagon. We have had two such lovely days and if tomorrow will only be as pleasant they could not have had a more favorable time for their trip. Pa wanted to get Jodie to stay with us at night but I would not let him knowing it would make it so hard for him as he would put in the whole day at hard work and then in all probability walk here and of course the walk to be taken next morning again and it was too much to ask of any one—and furthermore Mame and I thought it would be such a treat to be all alone for 2 or 3 days. And we have enjoyed it but we will be ready to welcome them home tomorrow. Jodie stayed with us Thursday night and walked down getting here about 9 o'clock—all were in bed but myself. He wanted Pa to get them some things. He said that his Papa wanted the family to come here in Feb. You may be able to come together if you think of coming in that month.

Won't it be jolly? It's a grand anticipating for us I can tell you. You just ought to hear the children talk. On the strength of Pa and Joe being away last night I had to tell a big story and you may know my theme was the return trip—your meeting us here etc. etc. And when I got through Kate said Mama that is just the gooddest story I ever did hear. Two bottles of medicine came this evening—(Arthur and Joe went to Theodore and got yesterday's mail) but no directions came—I suppose they will come in a letter from Annie. I don't suppose it will be necessary to take it unless I have another attack. I do not feel quite strong but I think it is partly from loss of sleep. Emma disturbs me frequently—also Joe's terrible snoring which I cannot get used to. I slept better last night than I have for a long time. Jim & I took the gun and went over by George Terro's to day but couldn't find any thing. Jodie sees a wolf once in a while. I am kind of bothered over Christmas. Don't know whether I had better go to Bowdle or have you send from Leb. I am half persuaded to go to Bowdle as I want to get candies etc. and I think Pa is such a poor hand to buy for poor folks. If he has plenty of money he can do as well as any body. We can easily tell in the mornings about what kind of a day it will be—I will run no risk and leave Emma and other children with Joe. I have sent for knives for the three boys, and I told Pa not to give over 30 cts. apiece for them. I do wish we could afford to get Jim a fiddle. Joe says Minwell Terro (14 years old) plays right nicely and uses his bow splendidly and I know he would willingly show Jim and like to. One of the older ones plays— but it may have been Joe, and he is the one who died a few weeks ago. Dont get this for Jim because I speak of it for I know how hard you are striving to keep us supplied. Jim would be pleased with a good little french harp and we can't get them here nor at Ipswich.

Kate and Emma want to have dolls of some kind—not expensive but cheap. A small bottle of perfumery would be nice for Mame as she is very fond of it and has none. I will go to bed now and so will bid you good night dearest.

Nov. 14

It is now 12-15 minutes.

The day is cloudy and wind from N.E. but it is not cold and Pa and Joe are liable to come in most any time. We are all respectable and I believe would pass for white folks should any one happen in. Mame and Emma are the only ones with me just now. I have jowl and bones on for dinner. Pa has been wanting the former ever since we bought the hog and he will be in good condition to enjoy it all the more after riding. Old man Johnson[2] came over yesterday to see if I wouldn't buy a little fresh "buttah" he had churned the day before. I told him I was not buying butter now. He was rather inquisitive and wanted to know if the men would

---

2 Andrew Johnson, probably. He was a neighbor about a mile to the east of the Drapers. Mr. Johnson's "buttah" evidently amused the family; he gets quoted several times in the letters.

be back last night. I says they may come. It made me a little uneasy until I went to sleep but that was not late. I put the revolver in a handy place. The women around frequently stay for weeks alone with only a baby for company. Arthur had a buckshot handy and I believe he would shoot should occasion require it. Arthur received Child's History of England through mail yesterday but I didn't see the address and don't know who sent it. He is very much interested already. So is Mamie.

I must go back to Christmas.

Please don't get me any thing but a stick of candy. You know I don't go any where and need nothing if I should. And I have no place for ornaments. Pa will enquire the price of candies so I will know whether to buy or have you send. If you want to send Pa & Joe anything, get 2 big red cotton handkerchiefs and I'll warrant their pleasure. *They wash easy too.* I am going to get a cocoanut at Bowdle. Some one will go next week for coal if weather is pleasant and we will get a few cranberries for thanksgiving. I told Jodie if he and his Papa would take dinner with us we would manage to have some Prairie dog any how. If the day is not too nice for work they will come. Joe will endeavor to get some grouse. How will that be with cranberry sauce? If you could get that game of letters like we once had it would be nice for this winter and would aid Jim, Joe and Kate in learning to spell. Joe spells first rate. He has commenced the multiplication table and is now on the three's. Jim knows through the 10's pretty well. My way of teaching I suppose is not modern but I will try to have them learn something as soon as Arthur comes to a stand in arithmetic and Pa cannot advance him, after reviewing he must take up something else but I don't know just what yet. He is very fond of Natural History and it is so easy for him it is scarcely a study. I will wait until Pa comes to finish my letter. Children are all in here now. Emma in Mame's lap. A few nights ago Kate told Jim to let her alone; he made her so nervous.

Nov. 16.

Pa & Joe got home last night or rather about 2 o'clock P.M. yesterday. They were in fine spirits having made a satisfactory trip. Tree claim all right. Pa will write you. He came home looking like a Georgia Major with new pants and overcoat and cap. The latter a fur bought at Bowdle & quite becoming. I told him to get it. It was $1.50 and he thought it was very cheap. He also got himself felt boots and overshoes—$2.75 price of outfit, I believe. Then he got himself and Joe a pr. of overalls & Joe bought a pr. of mittens and suspenders. He bought felt boots for Jim and Joe with arctic rubbers (the latter I will send back) and a pr. of heavy shoes, brass tips for Kate—he couldn't get felts for her. I think I will have him to get M & me a pr of felts before winter as we will have to have some others—we are wearing our best summer shoes now and they are light, but we don't go out very much and our feet never suffer. Mame has very heavy warm hose.

They also brought back 870 lbs. Coal and the heap is larger than you sent for 1000. I gave Pa the $50 and he told me he had spent it all but a few cents, and would give me items, etc., as soon as convenient. Of course I know it is all right but I can't see how he should have spent it all and it worries me—but Pa don't know it—and don't refer to it when you write. I suppose he does the best he can but I believe when money is plenty he spends rather freely, for he is so timid about speaking. I noticed it when I was with him at Bowdle. I do not like to complain the least of him (for he is so good), and don't speak of it to any body. In my next letter I can let you know how he spent it. He brought 100lbs. of flour back and a few other things. Of course the mules were some expense and I suppose he paid Terro's expenses. Well, it may not be so bad as it seems to me and I will not worry over it and hope you won't Pa is now up to Mr. J's—he and A. having gone this morning. He will hand Mr. J. the

16 dollars for me. I have $25 left. Don't send any more soon, and talk as if it was a little scarce. You make it too easy for us. Bless your heart—I know you are the best fellow in the world and I know all of this is a drain on your purse and I am so afraid it keeps you worried. Don't worry about our fare for we have splendid appetites and boss meals. You know deserts don't agree very well with me and we are all better off without them. I know Em's pumpkin pies were mighty nice and appreciate your feelings about us but we are doing finely. Pa brought a few cranberries that I will cook and save for Thanksgiving. The children were more than happy with the candy and figs and Pa brought a few apples. We ate some of the good cheese for breakfast and it was good. Pa got the knives—25 cts. for one and 30 cts. each for 2. So much for Christmas. I want to save some of the candy for Christmas. Pa got 1 long stick and I will get more before Christmas. I have to be . . . [material missing]

Tuesday—

Immediately after breakfast and Pa is anxious to be off. It is a good cloudy morning and we hope to get rain. Oats are up but rain would bring them out wonderfully. Joe will harrow his ground to day and finish his flax tomorrow. Elie and Pete are looking fine and doing fine. We hear they could be sold for $500 in Cass Co. about 200 miles north of here. May yet find a buyer.

Poor old Terro was brought by here under arrest yesterday on his way to Bowdle. We do not know the particulars, but understood he resisted the officer. They had 12 head of his cattle that had been mortgaged. I presume he refused to give them up.

I suppose we are his only sympathizers. But they are very poor and I believe he has been trying to do better for a while.

With much love,

Fannie

Lebanon, Mo
Nov. 17th 1886

Dear Jim and Joe

I received your good old letter and was glad to hear from you Arthur and Arch are writing to Arthur but they are done now. I and arch and arthur have been gone to school all day we have got four cats and we have tamed that old white tom cat and she is good old cat to have got our seller nearly done now arthur says in his letter that he wishes that papa was reelected yes he was elected for probate judge he beat 16 votes arthur is trying to work his example in arithmetic I am behind time now I mean I am last to get done with my letter well I am getting sleepy now to.

Your afectionate friend

Roy B. Herndon

Lebanon, MO Nov 17, 1886

Dear old pard[3]

I got your funny but [illegible] letter yesterday now sitting on a low seat by the table in the dining room writing to you did you get a letter from bird[4] He said he was going to write to you pretty soon whats the news from him? I haven't seen him for about a month [illegible line] but it was [illegible] one of them have you killed any jack rabbits yet I've

---

3 Partner. Archie Herndon, who, with his brothers and sister remained lifelong friends of the Drapers, is writing to Arthur.

4 Bird Dodd, a mutual friend.

scene [sic] them we had a big snow here the other day about 4 inches deep dug us a big cellar behind the old kitchen we've just got lots of apples now tell Jim mamma is awful proud of the stone he sent Mamma wants to see you all as bad as you do us I expect you said you hoped papa was reelected well he is the Republicans are gaining on the democrats have you seen any buffaloes I wish I could come out there I would just have lots of fun oh I am so glad you all are coming back in the spring we'll have more than honey old times ah you bet well just have a picnic have you really got a dirt floor to your house may be we'll go to the magic-lantern entertainment tomorrow night it is at Mr. Greenleafs all are invited I went hunting with a gun you said you would rather see us than any other boys in Lebanon I would rather see you than any boys in United States nearly. I skated on the pond this morning going to school not on my skates though. Barney is a beautiful horse now I ride him any where he's not half so fat and pretty as ribbon was though not quite I've got all of your letters put away in a box all but one the very first one you wrote I wish I had it. It got lost some way I can't see half as much fun as I used to when you were here I can see more fun with you than any boy I ever saw are you sick of Dakota Oh I wish I was out there I never saw a grouse in my life what kind of birds are they have you ever been boat riding on Swan lake The other day we killed a skunk at school and the boys that handled it had to get away back in the corner of the room it smelt so bad the girls had there hankerchiefs to there nose all the time the lead pencil was so short that I couldn't write with it very good this all the news aroun here so I will close so goodbye goodbye my dear old Pard and friend.

Jas Archie Herndon

Goodnight towo[sic] I am nearly asleep, two [sic]

Theodore Dak. Nov. 18 1886

My Dearest Charlie:

Pa is home again from his Bowdle trip getting here about 3 o'clock this afternoon. I am always glad when he gets back from one of his trips for we never know what may take place—still I never worry about him when he is away. I have to call on you for money much sooner that I expected as I am now entirely out—having given Pa 25 dollars yesterday. And he spent it all but $8 for coal, fruit, flour & felts & rubbers for Mame—Hotel bill and mules—also $2.26 for Mr. Johnson—elastic ribbon and Pos. stamps. He will return again tomorrow for more coal for fear the weather will grow worse instead of better and by borrowing 2 dollars from a neighbor he can bring back a ton. He will stay one night you know. I let Mr. J. have $16 as he wanted me to. He told Pa he thought he could soon return it. Now it is a little more than 18. Pa has given me full account of his Aberdeen trip and although I run over them hastily I rather think it is satisfactory and seeing expenses itemized, it seems a necessity and not so enormous as it first looked to me. I will send you an account when I feel more like writing and you can see for yourself. I feel well but somehow I am in no mood for writing and cannot say what I want to. The children amuse themselves in various ways. They play what they call Post office, and I got hold of some of their notes and you can form an idea of what passes between them during that play: These letters I send were not written in regular order as you will see by reading them. Kate takes an active part in her way.

Joe is now answering little Jim's letter to enclose in this. Tell Jim— big Jim—when he answers Jim's letter for him not to write such a long letter he might founder somebody. Arthur & Mame are reading the Youth's Companion together. Kate and Emma are asleep. Pa will sleep inside with Joe tonight and they are making preparations for bed. I received a good long letter from Aunt Neal[5] yesterday and it made me homesick. If I could only be with you! It is a shame to send off such a scrawl and so [illegible] but you will excuse me this time. Children join me in much love and many kisses to your dear self. Much love to Sallie, you and little ones.

Truly and affy—
Fannie Draper

Theodore, Nov. 22, 1886

My Dearest Charlie:

I am writing a note to enclose in letter to Jim from Pa. I may be able to write another letter this week and may not but thought I would be sure of this anyhow as Pa wants to go to the office tomorrow morning and get to day's mail if weather is so that he can. We are having a blizzard at last—but not so terrible a one as it might be as Joe easily made his way to the stable and back this morning and I can now look out from our South window and see the stable very plainly—yet the storm is not raging as it has been. It was blowing and sleeting and snowing all night. Pa thinks it will not last a greatdeal longer. The little birds are plentiful around and the boys *will* have their dead falls but only a short distance from the house. I have been out a little ways from the house and the

---

5 Fannie's mother's half-sister.

wind is terrific and when you face it with the snow in your face, it would soon be blinding. Our house is as comfortable as any one could wish. We can make it too warm in fact. And now we especially appreciate the storm room. I don't know how we would fare such a day as this without it. It would be very hard to make this room comfortable I imagine, and I don't believe we could so without a great deal of trouble in hanging up blankets and piling boxes against the door. Then the shelter is splendid for the East window and keeps the fine snow out which blew in all night because shutter was back. All are now around the stove excepting Uncle Joe and he has been off about an hour—looking after mules I suppose. He says the stable is very comfortable this morning. Pa says Joe keeps it in good condition all the time. I know he cleaned it out before breakfast this morning. The children have all been getting lessons this morning. I heard Jim and Joe a few minutes ago and Joe spelled two words that Jim missed. He spells splendidly for a little fellow, but don't speak of it so as to make Jim feel badly if you write anything about it for I believe he is naturally quicker than Jim. Arthur is in partial payments and he don't like it much. Mame has headache a great deal as she used to when attending school, and studies more than I want her too. But she is so afraid of not keeping up with the girls at home. And she is confident of going back in the Spring. I don't hear Kate regularly but she learns fast.

Pa thinks we have coal enough to last until middle of Jan. any how and I know we have flour etc. for 5 weeks or more so we are all right for the present you see. Emma troubles me so I can scarcely write. It is now after 1 o'clock and Pa has been out awhile and reports weather is so cold as fury and wind just from the North. Found Joe roaching and currying mules. If it don't get warmer I am afraid we wont get grouse for our Thanksgiving dinner. Our cranberries are already cooked & bottled. Pa couldn't get a coacoanut in Bowdle but got 2 lbs. of stick candy and I am saving the candy you sent by Thad. They thought you sent the stick candy that Pa got them. They had the figs too—and the peanuts Frank sent them. They ate the last yesterday. Tad came down last night for his mail and he says when the family come they will only stay a few months at the most. That his Papa has no intention of keeping the family here very long. Pa thinks Tad's surely mistaken. I got a good long letter from Aunt Neal a few days since and she still wants to get us in Col. Willis. R.J. has accepted John's offer and will move out in the Spring or Summer. I think I will be content when I get back to Mo. and I hope it will be best for us to return in the spring. I don't want to unless it is best, but Oh, how I will hate a longer separation. I feel as if I can't have you come and go away without us. I was a long time getting over it before, but we will see. I want to do what is best without any more sacrifices on your part. Tell me on private paper what you think. Love to all.

Affy,

Fannie

Theodore Dak. Nov. 24, 1886

My Ever Dear Charlie,

A veritable blizzard we have had! And Pa could not go to Theodore as he intended yesterday, which gives me time to add a few more lines. Mame and Arthur are washing dishes. Kate and Emma playing—Jim and Joe running in and out and each one taking his turn in shaking me and altogether it is pretty hard for me to collect my wits.

As nearly as I can tell the blizzard began about 10 o'clock Sunday night (which was bad enough) blowing and snowing—but increased to such an extent that by Monday night we were, or rather our house was snowed frozen up, so there was no way of getting out only by pounding and cutting and as there was no occasion for doing that we contented ourselves by sitting around a good hot stove and spinning yarns and then dropping off to bed, one by one, wondering how others were situated— feeling sorry for poor unprotected cattle and last but not least so thankful that we were among the blessed—being warm and comfortable with a store of provisions and fuel (many thanks to you old fellow). I realize more and more all the time how many, many blessings we have continually, and I meant to send an account of expenses to you in this letter and forgot all about it but I will do it soon—and I know you don't care particularly but I want you to see, then you will know our prices etc. etc. So you needn't say anything against my doing it. I think it is a good plan.

Children studying some, but a good deal of confusion, crowded as we are in one little room. I hardly ever sit down to nurse the baby that I don't have a lesson to hear. I have very few leisure moments.

Affy—

Fannie

Nov. 25.

Thanksgiving. Rather cold and somewhat cloudy. Pa and Joe have gone to Mr. Terro's to water mules. Boys out in snow. Emma and Kate romping around. The two former will go to Theodore when they return and I hope will have a big mail to be thankful for. I will be satisfied with a long letter from you. Arthur has come in and is helping Mame with dishes. We have not heard from Mr. J's folks since Sunday night and don't know whether they will eat dinner with us. We would love to hear from them. It looks something like snow and I am afraid our good weather won't last. Jack rabbit tracks have been discovered near the house by the boys and they want to get traps ready for night. Joe went out yesterday with the gun but was only able to be out a short time and wouldn't venture again. Nevertheless we'll have a good dinner. You bet!

Yours,

Fannie

The children are just wishing we had a telephone[6] between us, but I told them I was afraid you and I would get no work done if we had.

Nov. 25. Jodie has just come down and reports somewhat favorable concerning their cattle. Only 74 are missing but youngest calves in the herd were found all right so I suppose none are dead any how. It is presumed the missing ones have gone South and Mr. J., Mr. Tanner, Jodie and Thad start out in search of them this morning. Jodie says they will run no risk on account of blizzard, so Em must not be uneasy or over anxious.

Jodie and Thad undertook to go to Mr. Tanner's to water mules Monday afternoon—not being able to see 10 feet ahead of them and wandered off south of Tanner's, but finally, struck knowing ground and found Tanner's. Then after getting lost on going out again, were only able to reach home about dark—and found their Papa about ready to start out in search.

It was his loud hollowing the boys heard or in all probability they would have stayed out all night as they were not going in the direction of home.

Jodie reports cattle belonging to others 14 miles from here found

---

6 The telephone was invented in 1876, and by 1880 there were nearly 50,000 in use, so, though the children are fantasizing, this is no anachronism.

Emma, the youngest Draper child to spend the winter in Dakota, and her older sister, Kate, posed for this photograph a few years after the family's return to Lebanon, Missouri.

over in the gulches so then cattle will all be found without doubt. Two were here. Don't let Em worry there is nothing she should be over anxious about, but a greatdeal to be thankful for.

　　Affy,

　　Fannie

THE FAMILY IS PREOCCUPIED WITH *blizzards and Christmas in December. Worries about the Johnsons' cattle lost in the snow storms, the problems of negotiating the routines of homestead life under blizzard conditions, the virtues of living in a sod house under these circumstances receive much attention. Clearly, Christmas gets very satisfactorily celebrated.*

Nowhere do we get information about the actual dimensions of the living space in the soddy, but inside measurements of 12 feet by 24 square feet would be generous. That yields 240 square feet of floor space, a sizeable proportion of which is occupied by a large table, bunks, a couch, a cupboard, a stove, and assorted chairs. A grown person requires about 30 square feet to extend his arms in all directions and turn around, and every parent knows a child takes up even more space than an adult. Nine people were confined in this space, and for a good portion of the blizzard time, the three Johnson men stayed there, too. Despite such stresses, the letters indicate that the family experienced a reasonable measure of peace on earth during the Christmas of 1886.

The essential flaw in the arrangement, of course, is the fact that Charlie is not with his family. He was there for a month or more in the summer, but the need to earn a salary to assure cash flow to support the family was compelling. Charlie and the president of the bank, Mr. Greenleaf, were the only officers of the Laclede County Bank, and one or the other of them had to be there to keep the business open. Greenleaf's health began to fail in the summer, and he died just after Christmas, so that added a powerful reason for Charlie's staying in Lebanon. Add the impossibility of travel to Dakota during blizzard conditions, and it becomes clear that it was not feasible for him to spend more time there. With the morale in Dakota becoming increasingly shaky and with the job situation at the bank in flux, questions about the viability of the Dakota venture are becoming more and more insistent.

Dec. 5, 1886

Dear Papa

I wish you would take all of us home in the spring. Jody and Thad stayed all night here and they are here now Jim is drawing now. it is snowing now ive got a french harp now tell Aunt Sallie I thank her for that dress. Mame and Mamma is washing the dishes now. Good by.

Kate

Undated, Dec. '86?

Mr. Johnson has his cattle quartered at Mr. Tanner's [?] I suppose pretty comfortably. Rupert T. told Pa [illegible] that he thought those would now get through the Winter all right. I should think they were somewhat crowded [illegible] his number has been reduced to a greater extent that I supposed. Mr. J. will come to see us before leaving for Lebanon which will be on Jodie's return. I think too you might be able to make a living up here if you could keep the mules and be here yourself but I would hate to have to wait here a year for that time to come and then I'm afraid it would not pay you in the end. Winters *terrible* and mosquitoes all Summer & Fall. You know when Thad & Joe arrived here in April or May they found mosquitoes and they worried us until they were frozen up. And there is so much wind and so little that is desirable it seems to me. Yet your being here would put everything in a new light to me. I might be able to look with pity on a short lived mosquito.

Thursday morning

Quite a change since yesterday and looks as if a blizzard was in the air. We do so long for steady clear weather, if even it remains cold. Pa and Joe are out for hay and Joe wants to go to Theodore when he returns if the weather permits. Children are all busy—A. M. & Joe with the lessons and Jim writing a letter to his Aunt Annie. Kate and Emma playing horse or something. When you ask her who she loves she generally says "Papa" but sometimes Mama. A few days ago she kissed me twice in succession, and I says who was that kiss for, and she says "Papa." She can repeat almost any thing you say and is learning to talk fast.

You see that Kate's letter to Mary was written weeks ago. I thought I had sent it but overlooked it somehow. I suppose no great harm is done however but I like to treat the little fellows right about such things. I believe they are almost as fond of getting letters as older ones. Sometimes they make a big fuss here when they are disappointed in their letters.

Did Alice Buster go and live with Lottie? and where is Miss Mary now? Give her my love when you see her and tell her we all want to see her. Johnnie[1] is her Grandpa's girl now. She can say Miss Mary pretty well.

I would love so much to know *precisely* how you feel about having us come home. Sometimes I have a feeling (a kind of intimation) that you would prefer to have us remain here a year or so longer. I know of course you want to be with us too. Am I right? I wish I could see your [illegible] before sending this off—it may reveal something—but I will write another before many days. With much love for all loved ones, too numerous to mention besides a big share for your own dear self I am ever

Your Fannie

Joe is now writing to his Aunt Annie too. Arthur *may* write. We have been [sic] a kind of blizzard but is much lighter and signs of breaking away. So Joe will go to Theodore. They returned a few minutes ago and thought it would not *near* do for Joe to venture out but our weather sometimes changes here in the twinkling of an eye.

Fan

[Udated December card]

Charlie: Pa and Joe will start in a few [tear] Joe fearing it may be a long time before it [tear] the opportunity I will send a card any how. So far [illegible] an unprecedented winter. Jodie and Thad were here all day yesterday, not being able to do anything outside. Mr. J. left here the day before but I presume was unable to be out yesterday. Tad left to day

---

1 Nickname for little Emma.

This photo, taken long after the year in Dakota, shows Fannie and Charlie enthusiastically entering into the "Spirit of Christmas," just as they did under very difficult conditions years before in Dakota.

intending to meet Mr. J. somewhere with [illegible] two others and return with cattle. It is clear and wind from S.W. Good possibilities, and somethings may be accomplished before more severe weather to benefit cattle especially. Jodie and S. Hull have gone to the Ranch to get wire, posts, etc. if any thing can be done. For 2 or 3 days we have been snowed in—mighty bad, I can tell you. It is rather hard on the little folks.

Love to all

FMD

[Dec., 1886]

. . . a few days ago I lost my air pistol and day before yesterday I found it and I tell you I was awful glad. last night we got snowed in and this moring Uncle Joe took the broom and made a hole through the snow and crawled out he had left the spade out. Yesterday Mr. Hull came down here and brought his snow shoes and us Boys just had a dandy time on them to day is Sunday and Grandpa and Uncle Joe are reading the Bible and Mama is nursing emma and Mame and Arthur are writing letters and Joe is getting a Bible verse and Kate is [illegible] We are having a big blizzard now. Yesterday I got a letter from Bird Dodd. Papa a sod house is so warm that Mama says she wishes we could live in sod houses in Mo. we don't feel the cold in here. I said Uncle Joe left the spade out but he left it in the barn and he had to get the snow away from the barn door with his hands to get the spade. the other day Arthur got a letter from Arch Herndon and he wrote a verse to Mame and this is what he said apples are good but [illegible] good by we all send love to all

your son Jim Draper

Emma got hold of this letter and marked on it.

Dec. 7

Dearest Charlie:

Pa and Joe are about ready to start to Theodore and I will write hastily and enclose in Annie's letter from Mame. It is a lovely day. Every body feeling well but I am not very strong, not sleeping very well for several nights. Mr. Johnson has not yet returned with cattle so I have no news from them. Jodie left us last night but intends being back to night. I find that it will be too much for my strength to keep Mr. J. and the boys here and will have to tell them so. I hate it for I would like so much to accommodate them, but I know I ought not under the circumstances.

They are ready to go.

Affy,

Fannie

Thursday, [Dec.] 9

We have had an early breakfast. Pa & Joe are getting ready to go to PO and Mame and Jim are going along as it is a lovely day. Mr. Johnson & Jodie are by our South window counseling about work before they separate for the day. Tad went to Mr. Tanner's last night and will go after cattle. You see by this writing that every one gets in my [tear] occasionally I have a jog from some one.[2] Emma wants me too. I wish you could see the little darlling. She does love to talk of you. Christmas there will [be] something to do at Theodore & they want us to take part. Mamie may. I couldn't go and leave little ones. Good bye old dearest with my kisses from your wife and children.

This is my last scrap of paper and it has been on the floor. Excuse dirt.

---

2 Fannie is being jostled and interrupted by all the commotion around her.

Colorado Springs, Dec. 12th, 1886

Dear Fannie

Arthur and Ed[3] sent, by mail, yesterday two packages containing a knife for Arthur, a pin for Mame, a harp for Jim, a top for Joe, a set of dishes for Kate, a ball for Emma, and some marbles and cards for all of them. The pictures in the rolls are to paste on coal boxes etc., Arthur says. The boys are both very busy and asked me to write you a note. Everybody here is well except Ed who has been sick for several days. He's at work but does not feel strong yet.

Mother says tell Mary[4] she will answer her letter soon.

I have been helping Arthur in the office since I have been here and have not a great deal of time for writing myself, but have more than the boys do.

The girls send us Charley's letters and yours so we hear from you occasionally but nothing direct from him which is most wonderful as the boys say they have not written to him for a long time.

I hope you will have a nice time at Christmas and that the things from here and Louisiana[5] will reach you safe.

Love to all

Yours affectionately

Fannie L. Draper[6]

I forgot to say that the hdkfs. are for you.

---

3 Charlie's younger brothers who worked for the railroad in Colorado.

4 Mame.

5 Louisiana, Missouri, where Charlie's mother and sister Ann still lived.

6 Charlie's sister who, with another sister, Laura, homesteaded land in Colorado during this same period.

Theodore, Dec. 13, 1886

My Dearest Husband,

How very dearly I want to be with you just now, no one knows but myself unless it is you—and I rather suspect you could make a close guess. It is after 1 o'c p.m. and I am trying to rest before getting our second meal which I try to have at 3 but sometimes when it is not convenient for Pa and Joe we take a little lunch and dinner later in the day. Then Mr. J., Jodie and Thad have been with us more or less for 2 weeks and they can never or seldom eat until night. (Pa has just given up the ink so I will give up the pencil.) Mr. Johnson and boys left us yesterday to get bedding and some things they wanted from their house fully intending or expecting to be back by 8 o'clock, but did not come until 12 in the night having to dig shovels or something out of 3 or 4 feet of snow. They made very little disturbance, ate what they could find and made their own bed on the floor and crawled in. I was awake but said nothing and soon went to sleep again. You ought to see the biscuits I make when they are here. You would think a Reg. was going out on a 2 weeks hunt. And it almost exhausts all my strength by the time breakfast is done for you know how I manage hot biscuits. I generally had light bread for supper—would bake one day for the next as I was not able to bake enough in one day to last any longer. Just think of it! They took their bid to Rosetti's to day and I suppose go there to night. It is a relief to me, although if I were not so easily tired I would like to keep them for I feel so sorry for Mr. Johnson and he is so good himself. He brought me down 2 cans of fruit, some ketchup, part of a jar of applebutter, and a can of tomatoes and some evaporated apples. It is a nice present but every thing of the kind makes me homesick—for I think of all of Em's work in connection with them and know just how her heart must have alternated between pleasure and pain while packing them for her loved ones, and they seem almost too sacred to eat—but that sentiment will wear off—particularly when good things are scarce. Amongst them it is a 3 pt. can of strawberries that Thad wants me to make a short cake which I will do some of these days when they can have a little leisure to enjoy it. Joe has just returned with mules and wagon having helped Mr. J. about finding cattle, and as it is about 3 o'clock I will finish dinner.

It is night again—supper is over and dishes washed—children around the table as usual—Arthur is writing to Bird Dodd—Mame was sure trying to get Emma to sleep who is wanting me. Pa & Joe are near by—the latter chewing tobacco which he continually does, and has given up smoking.

Dec. 14

Emma was so fretful last night that I had to take care of her and put my letter by. I had a slight colic any how but a small dose of castor oil soon relieved me. Mr. J's folks did not return last night, and I suppose they are permanently located with the Rosetta family. Jodie stayed with Frank Hull in order for both to start early this morning to Bacon's for straw with which to cover shelter for cattle.

Joe intended to meet Mr. J. at ranch (which is near Terro's now) and go for brush today, but it is snowing and blowing considerably from the N.W. and is too bad for him to venture out. As Mr. J. was depending on Alie to work with jack I hardly think he will go without Joe. Their mules are *very poor* and just about worked down. Pete and Alie are holding their own Pa thinks—but he don't want them to do any thing outside of home and hates for Mr. J. to ever want them. Still he gets them occasionally as Joe and I talk for Mr. J.

Pa wants to help him too but he is so afraid of Pete not standing it—he is not so hardy as Alie.

It is about 11 o'clock now and Pa is thinking of going to Theodore about 12 if indications for clearing up are still good—the sun is trying to shine. Arthur went with Tad on a bob sled to Tanner's yesterday morning and killed a jack rabbit—the only one he ever shot at and of course it made him a little proud. His gun is excellent or he is a No. 1 shot as he never misses his game. Probably he has missed a bird or two. Oda Tanner sent Mame 2 pullets—but I am afraid we will have to eat them—as we have no place for them, but stable, and not much feed.

It is not very courteous to eat up a present but neither would it be to return it and if necessary we will choose the less of two evils. Arthur has just been to well for water and says he believes it is 28 below zero, but it is surely not so cold. We don't feel the winter in here, so don't get anxious and worry your dear sweet self about us for I believe we could keep comfortable if it were 50 below zero or even colder. So far I have never been so comfortably warm in the Winter. So much for a sod house. Neither have I ever before lived in so much dirt—another item.

Your good letters with one from Mrs. Waters came Saturday and I just feasted for awhile. Thank her ever so much and tell her I can easily stand all such surprises. Your good *private letter* I am not through reading yet. I am sorry there is no prospect of your coming before March but we will enjoy pleasant anticipations until then if nothing more.

Jodie thinks of starting home next week if not before. Still his Papa tells him not to be too [illegible], so there is a probability of his not going. He will get information and give you all you want concerning proving up—borrowing money etc. But I don't like to wait so long as we have to advertise 6 weeks in advance of proving up and it takes so much time. I am ready to make the best of everything but oh dear I want to be with you, you blessed old dumpling—I feel as if I cannot wait sometimes, but we will try and be patient. Take good care of your self. How is your cough this winter and your nose trouble you any?

Tom[7] is a brick, he knows who is worth loving. Children send much love and many kisses to "good Papa." Give much love to the many loved ones. How I want to see them. Mr. J.J., Tad and Frank H. are here and our house is full. I don't hardly know what I have said.

Truly & affectionately

Fannie

I have received two packages from Annie. 2 books in one & I can't get a chance to examine it. I tried to, & saw five Pencils, blank books & there is something else.

Pa only has 18 letters to take to office.

––––––––––––––

Dec. 18th (circa)

Charlie:

If it is cheaper to send us paper of this kind and you have it to spare, you may please as we use a good deal and will soon be out again. Mr. J's folks come along and make use of it sometimes. 2 young men have lately taken claims near Terro's and have built a shanty this winter.

––––––––––––––

––––––––––––––

7 Tom Monroe, Fannie's sister Sallie's husband.

Saturday 18

We are truly having another blizzard. It is worse than yesterday—having commenced yesterday morning it is still raging. Not being able to get out I know nothing of its coldness. The snow banks terribly at our South door and window and is taken away frequently. Joe has been a long time at the barn and had to dig his way in through 5 or 6 feet I suspect. Pa will not attempt to go to P. Office today and will hardly go now before Tuesday as he can then get Monday's mail. In that case my letter cannot go until Wednesday. You cannot get another letter from me before Christmas, if you get this, and I wish you the happiest Xmas imaginable—If you could only be brought by old Santa Claus what a blessed old fellow he would ever be to me. Oh, I look at A's & M's books last night—and one is Joe's Boys.[8] M will be delighted. Young Yagers is the other but I hardly think it the same that Arthur had at home. I believe it is a larger book. It is now night and table again surrounded. Joe got in all right between 2 and 3 o'clock but was covered with ice. Ice forms all over the face & icicles suspend from the lashes and whiskers and hair when you are out a few minutes and a hairy man is a sight to behold. It has been a terrible day out.

Joe thinks Mr. J's cattle can't suffer with what protection they have—although they are not done with it yet.

---

8 A Louisa May Alcott novel.

18 December

Dear Aunt Laura;[9]

I am glad you sent me my spoon. Jim is sick. Josie has to get supper all the time. Mame is well as a hog. Once Kate was sick and she eat her breakfast in bed and I beged to eat in bed. I have some little booties and Kate has a little shoping bag what an old woman brought us. I got a dollie and Kate has to and a nigger dollie and a white dollie. Mary sent Kate a picture that's got Tom Monroe & Mary on it. Kate's got a pocket in her dress. The leaves are blowing fine. Kate is turned to a hog. Jim is writing for me. Josie likes Will. Grandpa's name is Grand Pa and he is my Grand Pa.

Emma Draper[10]

December 19, 1886

My dear Son Joe:

I was so glad to get your nice letter which I think was nicely written. That was a nice Jack Rabbit you drew. I think Grandpa must stretch a rope from the house to the stable and then when a blizzard comes Mamma can sew an iron ring in the seat of Uncle Joe's pants and by putting the rope through the ring Uncle Joe cant be blown out of the way and get lost. It may be pretty hard on him when the wind is blowing hard but he will get there all the same. Mamma might fix all of you boys that

---

9 CC's sister.

10 Dictated letter from little Emma, transcibed, with some interpolation, by her brother Jim.

My dear Son Joe:

I was so glad to get your nice letter which I think was nicely written. That was a nice Jack Rabbit you drew. I think Grandpa must stretch a rope from the house to the stable and then when a blizzard comes Mamma can sew an iron ring in the seat of Uncle Joe's pants and by putting the rope through the ring Uncle Joe can't be blown out of the way and get lost. It may be pretty hard on him when the wind is blowing but he very hard the same. will get there all Mamma might fix all of you boys that way so she could tie a rope to you when you go out to play and then she can bring you in when she wants you. If Grandpa had a ring he could be tied on so old Pete couldn't throw him.

Your affectionate Papa

You boys must take care of Mamma & the girls

A picture showing the house in the foreground and the barn in the background. A rope extends from the house to the barn, and a bearded figure being blown by the wind is held in check by a ring sewed to the seat of his pants with the rope strung through.

way so she could tie a rope to you when you go out to play and then she can bring you in when she wants you. If Grandpa had a ring he could be tied on so old Pete couldn't throw him.

Your affectionate

Papa

You boys must take care of Mamma and the girls.

Dec. 19, 1886

MY DEAR KATE,

WHAT A NICE LETTER YOU WROTE. I AM PROUD OF IT. I CANT PRINT VERY FAST. OUR BLACK KITTY IS AT DOCTOR BARR'S SO WE CAN GET HER WHEN YOU COME HOME.

YOUR AFFECTIONATE

PAPA

Theodore Dec. 16 1886

My Dearest Husband:

I shall commence a letter and be ready when I have an opportunity to send which may not be until Saturday. Pa will go then if weather is favorable. A blizzard seems to be in the wind now. It is kind of sleeting and blowing and the wind from the East—a pretty good indication— and it is cold. I should think 15 or 20 below zero.

I never experienced such biting cold weather in Mo. as we have here and I was never so comfortable in doors. We don't know it is Winter, only from confinement and if you were here and we were alone with the children, and Pa & Joe in comfortable quarters, we could just have a spendiferous time and I could be Oh so happy—but—Well we are having a mighty dirty time to say the least. Our floor is simply black.

I am now trying to write and also get dinner. Have baked light bread and have some on the house cooling for dinner. Mr. Kerchoff has just come in for his mail. He has been telling the boys of a large white weasel he killed a few days ago. All of the fur animals here are white now. The jackrabbits are almost entirely white. I have not seen a white owl yet. I wish so much now that I had learned something of the art of taxidermy or had Arthur to before we left home—You know I talked of it.

Night is here again—Emma & Kate asleep. Mame Joe and Jim around the table. Arthur playing with Loll[?] Joe by the stove chewing away on his cud. Pa in bed and may be asleep. I hardly think it is 7 o'c. yet. By the way I found the clock key inside the clock. I suppose when I first looked it was fastened in the upper part of the clock. It is not running now as it needs oiling. I took the face off and oiled it with my finger but it only run a few days—of course there were parts of it that I presume got no oil. I will have to take a feather and try it some day. I have never been able to open the top drawer of the machine and think the oil can is in it.

Do you know why Arthur[11] sold his house? You wrote as if it may have been sold by some one, but I hardly think you meant that. Probably Mother[12] was tired and wanted to return home any how. I do hope she and Fannie had a good time.

---

11 Charlie's youngest brother.

12 Charlie's mother, Sarah Fentem Draper.

Joe hauled hay for Mr. J's cattle again today—He learned from Robin or Tad through Robin's letter that Mr. Greenleaf was quite sick. I hope he is better and up by this time. Give my kindest regards to him and family including Mrs. H. when you see them.

Also remember me to Miss Mary and how is she getting along. I so often think of her.

The coasting here would be splendid now if we only had sleds—the snow is so firm—yet it would be pretty cold. A few days ago a Scandinavian stopped in to get some milk and rest on his way to Bowdle, having come 16 or 18 miles that day on snow shoes. They were made of pine and about 6 ft. long—he used a long upright stick on either side as supports and went along pretty fast although the snow was melting some. He said it was no work when the snow was hard and one could go very fast. Our boys tried making somekind [sic] afterwards but they were too short to work well without the right shape. It is snowing or sleeting to night but the wind is not blowing much. Joe thinks in 2 or 3 days Mr. J. will have shelter complete for his cattle. he will give him some help tomorrow with our team. Says Alie & Pete are doing nicely. They have excellent care and Joe keeps stable in good condition and is a right cozy stable after all.

The privy was never finished but we get along better than you might imagine.

I am training Emma who never wears "didies" now and continues to go barefoot. But she is just the sweetest thing and loves dearly to talk of "Papa."

How I wish you could come in and take her up by surprise. I am sure she would know you. The children never get tired of talking about "good old Papa."

Arthur has just gotten out of bed and dressed because he says he cant go to sleep.

I wanted to see what Annie had sent and had the boys go to bed.

I make them go to bed every night. I believe they would draw or play the whole night if I didn't.

[A portion of this letter is missing.]

. . . be best for us to wait and go with them but oh me! how long it will be to wait. Yet we could save about $100 but would we feel paid in the end? It is a long time to wait and a long tedious trip to make— but the time is all I would hate about it—and getting black[sic]. I wouldn't mind the trip a greatdeal. Let us know as soon as you can what we must depend on (if you can) and then I will do my best to be reconciled and not complain.

Joe will go to Theodore in a few minutes and I am expecting a letter from you and dont want to detain him. I would have finished my letter satisfactorily last night if Emma had behaved herself. Clara wrote Mamie there was a great deal of pneumonia in town. Do be careful old dearest and don't leave the bank when you are over heated. Take care of any cold you may possibly have. You need me there to look after you I know. The boys are at work with the firecrackers already. Just after breakfast. They have more fun that you can shake a stick at.

Sat. at Theo. thermometer down to 40 below 0.

With mush[?] and kisses

Fannie

You were mistaken in sending me a draft of $25. You forgot to sign it.

Walworth County Dakota, Wednesday 22 Dec. 1886
10 a.m. Just after breakfast
CCD

Dear Friend

We all did justice to breakfast. Joe is going to ride over to P.O. for turkey for Christmas dinner. We received letters yesterday; from you to Fannie; Clara to Mamie; Jimmie to me, from Marshfield. We all mourn the loss of Mr. Greenleaf and sincerely and deeply sympathize with his bereaved wife and children. But the ways of God are past finding out. He gives and he takes away. "Blessed be his name." Fannie is writing you. Joe is waiting. I will write Jimmie shortly. I think he is improving his business prospects while doing well for the times. Tell him to take calomel for sick headache.

We can at once see that Mr. G's death will work changes and most likely you will be induced, almost required, to remain in Lebanon. You will be almost a necessity there. You will inform us. Much love to all.

Truly & affly
JW McClurg

Theodore, Dec. 25, 1886

My Dearest Husband:

You see what night it is and I have had a sweet melancholy Christmas, but a happy one.

Can you understand me? Melancholy, because you were not with us and I would find my mind wandering back to other Xmas's which you and I have had so happily together with our little ones and don't you know it would bring a sigh or a heartache. And yet I have been happy in the children's pleasure, for I can truly say they have had a jolly Christmas. And to begin with Christmas Eve I never saw Emma in such a mood. She had a short nap during the day and at bedtime seemed to have the Spirit of Christmas Morning and Mame and I sang—played and worried with her until late and finally lay down with her and then she wanted to sing loud and there was great danger of waking Joe & Kate, and so my Santa Claus work had begun. I was somewhat "previous" but she finally succumbed and Mame and I fell to work with a zeal and you can imagine what passed better than I can describe. You may well know how cautious we had to be under the very noses of the little ones and were late in getting to bed. Poor little Mame wants to share anything that looks like trouble with me yet she rather enjoyed last night's work. While sitting with Emma & waiting I had to shed a few tears over memories of the past and your absence but Mame didn't know it and she soon had a pleasant time of disposing of the packages and sometimes I was considerably addled to know just where to assign this or that. If old Santa Claus hadn't been so liberal I would have had no trouble and the children probably as happy. In fact they floor was almost covered and I was surprised at the quantity when I saw such a spread.

Dec. 27

How rapidly time flies—but not too much so for me now. Christmas morning was a duplicate of those gone by with the exception of your dear self not being with us & Pa and Joe in your stead. Our little fellows were on the alert early catching Christmas gifts[13] and rousting "Uncle Joe." It was hard to make them wait the fire and they would hop up and down and take a peek now and then and mention some article they had seen. Kate couldn't contain herself at all but was all excitement; and when they got at their stockings and things what shouts and laughter followed you can better imagine. Santa Claus was indeed liberal to us. Joe's top is a beautiful large humming one and very musical. Emma's ball is a large japanese with painted, raised fancy figures over it and has a whistle of course. Jim's harp is a double one and he says the best he ever had. It is very sweet. Arthur's knife is a Westenholm with four blades and he is very proud of it. Mame's pin is beautiful and the kerchiefs for me are all that I could want. All are hemstitched and they are embroidered. They sent a quantity of marbles—glass-crockery, stone. A game of letters which I gave to Jim, but we have all forgotten just how to play it. There are dol. marks & nos. on some of them, & I believe altogether there are two sets. The hoods did not get here—Joe had gone to day for Friday's mail. We were having a blizzard Friday and Saturday and Sunday it was very cold—It is probably warmer today as it is very bright and still. Kate's dishes, I was about forgetting—they are pewter I suppose—but quite large and mighty pretty. Her doll of course she is very proud of but Emma wants it all the time as she doesn't care as much for hers. The pistol I gave to Jim and it is the apple of his eye which makes me glad you sent it. The

---

13 This refers to an adaptation of the old Southern antebellum plantation tradition involving servants or slaves surprising their masters on Christmas with the "Christmas Gift" shout, after which the master was obligated to present a token gift. The custom evolved into a kind of "one up" game played out on Christmas Eve and Christmas morning within the family, even to this day.

harp I gave to M & A & they were tickled not expecting any thing of the kind. I also gave the penwipers to Mame thinking it too cute for one of the boys. Emma loves the ring and bear. All delighted in the candy and nuts—the latter particularly being such a treat as the English W. and filberts are almost unknown to our children. I can testify to the good quality of them all and none are the least strong. My leggings will come in handily. Mame and I will make good use of the pretty [illegible] and I am wearing one in my flannel dress now—having put both on Sunday for the first time. I am proud of my comfortable flannel dress and think almost too much of it, to wear it in this dirty place, but I wore my old black skirt in perfect rags in front before I laid it aside. I could see that Pa was proud of the thermometer as well as his candy & nuts, (I made him hang up his socks) Santa Claus brought "Uncle Joe" a plug of tobacco, bunch of firecrackers, candy & nuts and he was pleased, too. I gave Kate one of the knives as she particularly requested Santa Claus up the stove pipe to bring her a knife and pencil and got both. They like the tablets & pencils & chewing gum. I got 15 cts. worth of apples and put one for each of them in their stockings. And last but not least are the books. Arthur was very much pleased with his, apparently meeting an old friend and was soon going over old familiar ground and having a good time. But "Joe's Boys" just the book Mame was wanting most and she was one of the happiest and proudest of girls when she read aloud the title. She almost read it, but is now going over it again and reading aloud to Arthur and Jim is a listener most of the time. We have had a good Christmas but you may sure know old dearest that you were talked of more than once and if my thoughts were written that were given to you and other loved ones of Lebanon they would fill a book.

We were disappointed in not having Mr. J. & boys here Xmas nor were they here yesterday (Sunday). We had a good dinner—turkey nice and tender—jelly and hot rolls—corn & tomatoes, butter & splendid gravy. I could get no egg for cake but had ginger snaps. And no one missed cake & pies. We got nice sweet milk from Mrs. Terro which Mame & I particularly enjoyed as we drink neither tea nor coffee for dinner or supper. I do hope you had a happy Xmas. Poor Mrs. Grumley I know it was a sad one to her and Mary.

I am anxious to hear from you and learn something definite as to our plans—whether the prospect for going home is any better and whether you will try to run up here in the Spring if not sooner. If you take charge of the Bank for Mrs. G. I don't hardly see how you can get off. Pa will write to Carter (for me) tomorrow and ask some questions as to what is necessary about proving up and whether it can be done in your absence. You know it will do us no harm to learn—and then should you want to or any thing of the kind we will know what can be done. Probably you have already written to him concerning those things. Pa thinks the prospect for returning home is better and I really think he is not much in favor of remaining a great while himself after he can prove up. That is if we return & Em's family never comes. Thad was over a little while this evening and said his Papa was going to try to prove up without his family when he returned after Feb. He also said Jodie had given up his trip home until March. Poor Jodie—I know it has been hard for him—for it has been a long cherished hope with him.[14] I have been thinking if we return in the Spring—we might be thinking to leave the mules for Pa & Joe to use on both places so they can return to Mo. by

---

14 Bureau of Land Management records show that only Charles Draper and Joseph (Jodie) Johnson were ever actually issued patents, although the letters talk of Joseph McClurg (both father and son), Marshall Johnson, and Thaddeus Johnson having planned on "proving up."

wagon in July or August. Pa says they could get back with an expense of $25 he knows. It might . . . [Remainder of the letter is missing.]

---

31 December, 1886

My Dearest Charlie

Jodie expects to make a start for Lebanon in the morning and although I have nothing to write I must send a few lines any how or I am sure you will be disappointed.

I cannot tell you how he made arrangements for going home. A few days ago his Papa didn't see how it could be accomplished they were so terribly pressed for money. Probably he intends borrowing more on his place. He was only here a short time to day the first we have seen of him for a week or more and we were so surprised—but glad that he is going home. I think he means to put a Spider in Dean's dumpling[15] if there is half a chance—whether he wants to marry Kate or not himself.

It makes me homesick to know of his going back and I even dread to see him in the morning. If there was only a prospect of our being with you soon—oh my, how would we feel though! Tomorrow begins another year and if it were not for keeping Pa awake we would sit up with the old year—who has really been a good friend after all. The children and I never want to go to bed but I often feel the need of sleep. Pa wants us in bed by 9 o'clock and it often goes against the grain of us Drapers. We are having very cold weather again. In the shade it must be 25 or 30 below 0. Kate and Joe were very proud of their nice letter and Kate took possession of

---

15 A "spider in a dumpling" signifies a secret poisoning.

it. Be sure and write to Jim soon. I am afraid he is a little jealous and I think he is writing to you now. I have a large beef heart that I intend to stuff and cook tomorrow and then I can have an apple roll or some kind of pies. Wont you come over and eat dinner. Oh it will be good. Pa has been in bed quite a while. Mame has Emma on her lap and is sitting near "Uncle Joe," Arthur, Joe and Kate and talking and doing almost everything. Some times they get a little yarn out of big Joe to the children's joy and delight. The children have not been studying any for two weeks, of course I could not expect anything of them this week and somehow they seemed too excited last week and I had to let them off with fair promises to begin in good earnest next Monday.

While I think of it, did you ever send the 6 cts. to Mr. Youky—or whatever his name is for sending Mame's sunbonnet?

I am anxious to get another letter from you but hardly expect to until Monday or Tuesday but possibly may.

Somehow I have been more lonely since poor Mr. Greenleaf's[16] death.

This country looks so desolate now—still the evenings (when clear) are beautiful indeed. I go out sometimes and gaze around but can't stand it long, it produces such loneliness. But in doors I feel much more at home, if it is dirty.

The cupboard is about half way between the stove and bunks on the right as you face the stove and looks pretty well. Kate would have her house in there and that sets near the head of her bunk. If there was anything else nice about this room I would tell you but there is nothing worth mentioning. The clock shelf is on the left of the cupboard with a

---

16 George Greenleaf was the president and owner of the Laclede County Bank where Charles was cashier.

Fannie's note included with Kate's work reads, "This is Kate's gotten up letter and in spite of dirt I have to send it."

few things on it beside the clock.

I must take Emma as she is beyond Mame's control. Love & kisses from all of us.

Truly and affy

Fannie Draper

Dec. 31 1886

Dear Papa

I got your letter day befour yesterday. I got a knife and a pencil

Xmas and two bunches of fire crackers and a nice big huming Top. and I can hit it on top and it will go a different sound and an old man and a old woman to fit on top of it and when it spins the old man and woman dance. me and Jim have got a pair of snow shoes.

good by;

Joe Draper

Part Six

JANUARY AND FEBRUARY, 1887

JANUARY AND FEBRUARY WERE CLIMACTIC MONTHS *for the enterprise. All the themes come to a head during those months. Matters of household economy; the fate of the mules (and the fascinating issue of the tender treatment of those delicate beasts); the transcendent importance of letters from home; the blizzards, of course; bank politics back home; and morale, in general, are all substantially developed in these letters.*

The most critical issue, though, is the residency requirement for proving up and the stern judgment of Carter, the attorney, about the necessity of Charlie himself personally living on the place for six months. Fannie is outraged that the effort and sacrifice she and the family had invested counted for nothing.

A key assumption to this point had been that all would be well if only Charlie were there with his family in Dakota. In a letter to Charlie, the Governor lets drop, however, that "I think they [the Draper family] will not be contented to remain here without you and probably even with you . . ." So, the enterprise is pretty nearly doomed, it would seem. The way Fannie processes her brother Jim's suggestion that she lacks grit adds an interesting shading to that question.

Jan. 4—1887

My Dearest Husband:

I have just sent all of the little tads away from the table that I might be able to write you a more decent letter. The little coons didn't like it, but now they are having a good time listening to some talk from Arthur. When all are around the table no place will suit Emma but on the top of the table just in front of me. Mame has the headache and can do nothing with her, so I will have to take her after all. As good luck would have it, Emma nursed and went right to sleep. Sometimes she will take an hour's nap and wake up and not go to sleep for 2 or 3 hours. She is learning to talk pretty fast, occasionally will put two words together. She is an affectionate, generous little thing and thinks any ailment can be cured with a kiss from her, and she loves Kate dearly but annoys her a greatdeal taking her playthings at every chance. Kate thinks a greatdeal of a little mug you sent Xmas. One I gave to her and the other to Emma.

I received your nice letter written just after Xmas today. I tried Xmas day to form an imagination concerning your spending Xmas. I hardly thought you would work all day and I never thought of your taking dinner with Jim. I am so glad Santa Claus remembered you. Joe envies you of those nice cigars, nevertheless Santa brought him a plug.

Mame sent her toboggan cap to Clara W. to day. She probably would never wear it and we thought it a shame to pack it away, when we knew it would be so becoming to Clara and Mame was more than desirous to send it. Clara has done a greatdeal for her you know and Mame has done so little in return. You had better not speak of it to Em's folks for fear it might get to Aunt Neal[1] and I should hate that.

---

1 A sister of Fannie's mother who, apparently, had given the toboggan cap to Mame as a Christmas gift.

In your letter you spoke of having sent two $25 drafts—did you send them together? I got one. Sometime in last month, I do not remember the exact time but before the 20th, and it may have been towards the beginning—I cant just remember, but I was sure I acknowledged it. I have received none since. In your last letter you spoke of having sent one but it has not come yet. I suppose it will yet come. Jodie said his Papa would go to Bowdle shortly (on Saturday last) and he has $5.00 and a memorandum to make use of for me. I have yet a little left. We live on bread, flour, meat, coffee, beans, tomatoes, sugar, and fruit and rice. You see we are not at the point of starvation yet. Since becoming accustomed to coal I like it first rate. Joe manages to get scraps of pine for kindling, with hay. He often gets after our boys for getting his kindling. I am so glad you think Hoskinson[2] and his party stand the best chance of getting the Bank, for they have been my choice—looking from it from our stand point, which may be somewhat selfish. I feel as if either other party should get it, your situation would not be so permanent. I know you will get a good thing. Poor Mr. Greenleaf, he was a good friend after all. What has become of Robin? Will he get a place again? I suppose you will see Jodie this week sometime, but on account of snow banks he did not reach home to day as he expected. Probably he can give some good advice concerning our claim. It seems to me I had rather borrow money here than there, if I gave the claim as security, but you may be able to get some other way. I am trying to be patient but you and home are scarcely ever out of mind and I cant prevent it—when I go to sleep or lying awake at night—the first thing in the morning and so on during the whole day. Everything is still white with snow and of course will remain

---

2 Isaac Hoskinson, a prominent Lebanon entrepreneur, owner of the Lebanon Woolen Mills.

so until spring. There are drifts in front of the stable above any man's head, and it is hard and compact so we can walk right over it.

Mame is now telling Kate about a trip we will make back home and is making a jolly thing of it. The boys are talking. Joe has put down his paper and is chewing his cud preparatory to going to bed. Pa has been down for more than an hour. He felt real sorry to see to day, that Gen. Logan[3] was dead.

I was forgetting to speak of New Years. I got out a package of candy that I had stowed away, to the great delight of all, and it made it seem like a festive day. Then we had a dish of beef heart which was mighty nice indeed and if we ever get home I intend to cook one as we had it here and see what you think of it. Currant Roll was our dessert but it was good. I cannot send this over until Thursday so I will not finish to night.

Wednesday about 2 o'clock:

It is blowing and snowing terribly and Pa and Joe have gone for hay and I am afraid they will suffer but probably they will not [illegible] to bring hay. It was not near so bad when they left—still they were well provided.

Mr. Johnson has not returned that money, but it will not be necessary. We will get a ½ of beef from them to day and that will leave us 2 or 3 dol. in their debt when we settle. The hay will have cost us $2.00 per ton—just what it cost them. I do not know just the quantity we have engaged, but more than $25 worth. $2 of the 16 they returned. Pa thinks

---

3 John Logan of Illinois had served in U.S. Congress with McClurg and later distinguished himself as a division commander at Vicksburg and Atlanta during the Civil War. After the war, he served as U.S. Senator from Illinois.

time- You, Jim and Joe have just gone. Katie is preparing,
____ is asleep, Arthur & ____ Mama are talking by
the stove - I hear Clara's name. They never want to
go to bed. We will be snowed in again by morning but
we get fresh air from the east window. Friday night !!.
You wouldn't begin to know our place if you were dropped down near it the snow and high drifts so greatly
changes the appearance of all surroundings. A little
distance from the house towards the stable it looks
something like this if I can make you understand.
You know I can't draw _____ the window
that shows is South _____ and belongs
to our room that you _____ floored.
The part all snow is the addition and d is an opening

of the roof is visible. The ravines are wonderfully
filled up. And you can scarcely tell where the barn
is, as the snow is about on a level with it towards
the ravine. Joe was most of the day digging the wagon out of the snow preparatory to hauling hay to morrow
If we had made a sled the beginning of winter it would
have been the thing- but probably now by the time we
could get lumber the snow will be leaving us. I am afraid
he will have a hard time tomorrow. And he wants to go to P.O. if we can
also. I am so sorry I couldn't get my letter off before but it could
not be done. Pa & Joe & Emma are in bed. ___ is writing. A & Jim
playing chequers. Joe & Kate drawing. Kate drew these pictures
in her letter to you. She never wants any one to give her any help
and she is very quick. She is so fond of chequers that she has
been neglecting her lessons lately. Joe McC. is the only one who never
____ Pa is about as fond of it as Kate. Mr. J moved himself
____ a day or two ago to mr. Sannies- or it was his intention
____ lizzard may have prevented. I am so very glad you antisip
____ ____ then you can be with us more and I hope
____ ____ 5 you desire

Fannie was apologetic about the quality of her drawing of the soddy buried in snow.

the mules did at least $10 worth of work. The beef we get at 7 cts. and I suppose there will be at least 100 lbs. If we could get pork I would prefer it as it is cheaper, but we can't until some one goes to Bowdle and no telling when that will be.

I don't doubt that Mr. Johnson will want the mules frequently again and we want to accommodate him when we can, but they are so hard on a team that Pa don't like to give Alie and Pete to their charge at all. At one time their poor little mules begged out for awhile. And last Fall Pete gave out when they had him but seemed somewhat weak before. By more feed and good careful management he came out all right and is perfectly stout now and as free going as ever. But I am almost sure he would have been dead if the Johnson boys owned them. Pa and Joe came back all right but pretty cold.

6. *Thursday*

Pa and Joe have gone after hay again. It is a bright, cold and still day. It must be 25 below 0 outside. Joe cannot go to Theodore today but Mr. Hill is in the country and I may be able to send my letter by him and want to get ready.

Pa took your letter (to Mr. J. to read) that referred to getting money for him, and he said he did not seem disappointed. He has just received a letter from Mr. Shubert[4] promising him money very soon or right away. Mr. Shubert owes Pa something.

Mr. Hill has come.

———————————————

4 Mr. Shubert was a former employee of McClurg's at the business in Linn Creek.

Jan. 10, 1887

My Dearest Charlie:

I write so often and have so little to write about and I know they (my letters) must be somewhat monotonous—at the same time I know you cant hear any too often if you feel as I do about you, and I flatter myself you do. I probably cannot send this letter before Thursday or even Saturday, but I like to commence so as to have plenty of time and not be hurried and I have to allow for many interruptions. Emma is now crying for me and I generally have to take her when she begins fussing for me as nothing else ever satisfies her. The children have the couch and are all right near the stove—yarning. Jim playing his harp. Joe is reading near me—and Pa has been in bed a few minutes—It cant be 7 o'clock yet.

The $25 draft came Saturday after circling around about 3 weeks. You had put Mo. on the envelope instead of Dak. And it had gone to the Inquiry Div. In St. Louis. I had not particularly needed it. But we will have to have coal before a great while and probably next week Pa and Joe will borrow Mr. Johnson's bob sled and go for coal and also get provisions that we will want then.

You did not enclose a draft in my letter for Mr. Johnson as you said you would but you may have sent it to him. We have not seen him for 3 weeks or more. Thad runs over occasionally for something. Of course you have had a talk with Jodie by this time and probably will know whether you think best to borrow money up here. Don't do it unless you want to, for if you think best I am willing to stay here longer but don't know how I can possibly stand it, but will try if you say so, for your sake.

I know I was anxious to make the move and now I feel as if it were a great mistake and whether it is a duty to stay here and make the best of it (if we can get away without too much expense) I don't know. I am sick of it—and there is no prospect of you joining us. Even if we go home how can you come for us? It may not be necessary if we can prove up without you but wouldn't it be jolly—all going back together? And wouldn't I prepare a nice big lunch and we would only have coffee and tea to buy.

Saturday I received your letter written Sunday night and after your busy day. Of course I was considerably disappointed that Hos. & Co.[5] did not take the bank and if I had been with you I would have said hold off awhile (even if other party should want you) in view of another bank starting. And if you have not got the position under D. & O.[6] don't feel despondent for if the other bank don't start you will have an offer from some one if Mrs. G.'s[7] matters are not enough for you. Will that occupy much time? I am glad you have the Insurance.[8] I will use all the economy I can and we wont begin to starve on it either—now don't think we will live on air and water for I assure you we will have enough and to spare. You would enjoy eating with us if you were here now. We have nice beef. I have had Emma twice since writing this and only got her down a few minutes ago. The boys have just kissed me good night for you and myself. (A. and Joe) Jim always kisses me and then faces Lebanon and kissing his hand says "good night Papa" and I believe he never forgets it. I love to see him do it—he is always deliberate. Mame seldom fails to kiss me good night for you. You would know you had been a good Papa if you could hear these children talk.

---

5 Hoskinson.

6 Diffenderfer and Owens.

7 Mrs. Greenleaf, the widow of the bank owner for whom Charlie had been cashier.

8 Charles sold insurance for Hartford and Aetna at various times. See his evaluation of the life of an insurance salesman in the letter to Governor McClurg, June 8, 1887.

This photograph of the 1948 blizzard at the Bietelspacher farm, near the site of the Draper homestead, is a stark reminder of winter on the Dakota prairie. Photo courtesy of Audrey and Dennies Bietelspacher.

Jan. 11

If you think best for us to return in the Spring do you want to sell Pete and Elie? We have had no offers, but Mr. Tanner wants to rent some land to Joe to be put in oats (as he doesn't want to farm this year) and Joe can do nothing of the kind without a team (I think Pa will write you about it). I feel so sorry for Joe & Pa if they remain up here. At the same time Mr. J. and Jodie have told them to come and bunk with them and they can help each other in various ways if we go home. I intend to let Marshall know how Pa is situated. I know Mr. J. can let them have oxen but they will have to break them which will make work very slow and not near half could be done, as by the mules. At the same time I am sorry

for you and feel that you want to get rid of the mules if you can at fair figures for they might die on our hands (but they can't be in more careful
hands) and the debt would be yours all the same. The worst feature about
selling in the Spring (if we go back) is this, it seems to me. If there is another drouth Pa & Joe will want to prove up and get out. And then, if they
have the mules and wagon and good luck, $25 will take them back and
you may be able to get as much for the mules near home. This is probably
useless talk—but it is often the case, and will do no harm I hope. I wish
we could see each other a talk over everything. Do you want us to stay up
here? Frank writes as if they are coming. I think—oh how blind! And they
will find it so when they are here and unable to get away. Tell Em I say—
never to come unless Mr. Johnson *insists* on it, for I know she can't help but
regret it most terribly. She thinks now it would be a relief from certain cares
and vexations and it probably might for a little while—but she would find
it brief indeed, and would rather be back on the old farm living on bread
and water and would be willing to dress on cottonade and calico rather
than remain here—and particularly if Mr. Johnson spends most of his time
there. "Distance lends enchantment" is only too true.

Jan. 12

I don't know whether I can write any thing to night but as Joe will
go to Theodore tomorrow (if he can) I will finish any way. Joe is near me
patching his mittens and the children are every where—Grandpa playing with Emma. He loves Emma and of course she loves him and likes
to sit in his lap. We are having some kind of blizzard—wind from the
East (always bad) and some kind of snow; but we have to go out to realize it. It is so very quiet in here—that is no outside wind or noises to any
kind affect us in here—and sometimes when I go out it seems almost like

a surprise to see so much snow everywhere, and have your eyes shut almost instantaneous by the mist and wind. It is cutting I can tell you and almost takes your breath away. Pa saw Mr. Johnson yesterday and he had received your draft. Marshall wrote there is a prospect of getting Robin a situation in a Carthage bank. I hope he will. Four more of Mr. J's cattle have died. I believe 3 were smothered somehow and one choked himself being tied. Poor fellow, he seems unlucky. Mr. J. not the steer. Don't tell Em as he may not want her to know. Tell Jim to try drinking hot water before each meal and it may prevent his headaches if he will also be careful of his diet. If you never sent for . . . . [remainder of letter missing]

Jany 9 1887

My Dear Jim:

I received your good letter some time ago. I will send you the caps for your pistol. Tom[9] said a speech tonight before going to bed. This is the speech:

> *Wake up boys, wake up!*
> *I am about to make a speech,*
> *And I want you all to hear me.*
> *A frog is a mighty funny thing.*
> *When it stands it sits.*
> *When it runs it jumps.*
> Then Tom made a big jump.

---

9 Whether Tom is a cat or a frog or something else, we do not know.

I must soon answer Kate's and Joe's nice letters. I hope your kitty catches all the mice. I think old Santa Claus was mighty good this Christmas, don't you?

Give my love to Arthur and Mame and Joe and Kate and Johnny [Emma] and Mamma and Grandapa and Uncle Joe and yourself and Uncle Marshall and Tad and Alie and Pete and Prince.[10] I am not acquainted with your kitty or I would send my love to her.

Cant you boys catch a few gophers in the spring to bring home as presents to some of the boys? They would like it. Our old Black Cat is still around I learn waiting for us to get home. Will you boys forget how to climb trees by the time you get here? You must all study hard so as not to be behind the others in your classes. I think Arthur and Uncle Joe might find some Jack Rabbits these moon-light nights. Jodie says that was a splendid one that Arthur killed. I have been working very late every night for some time and it is about twelve o'clock now.

Affectionately, your

Papa

J.S. Carter

Attorney at Law

Aberdeen, Dak. Jany 15th 1887

J.W. McClurg

Theodore Dak.

Dear Sir:

It will be necessary for Draper himself to reside on the tract at least

---

10 Elsewhere, Governor McClurg mentions Prince, and, according to Arthur's cartoon, a dog was a member of the party that left Lebanon. If he was actually a part of the household, he receives no other mention in the letters.

six months before offering proof.[11] Notice to make such proof and publication of notice may be had before the expiration of the six months. Draper must be personally present when proof is made. The notice of intention to make proof may be signed by him any where.

Yours Truly,

J.S. Carter

Jan 16th 1887

At home on the Farm.

Dear James

Well Jim I am going to write you tonight. How do you like Dak.

I think I would like it I know I would like to kill the game. My bird-dog is a big dog now and can set quails. Charley and I have caught and killed 70 rabbits and 3 pole-cats and hope to catch more. I have 14 guineys and a lot of ducks. If you come back before we go up thare I will give you a pair of each. What did you get Xmas. I got a gold pen and a hawk-bill knife. Tell Arthur I will write him in a day or so. Jodie is with us now he thinks town is awful dull he would go back right now if he had the money I wish I could go back with him, but I cant

Thare don't any of us go to school but Charley and he only started last Monday. I think Charley is going to write to Joe before long. It is about bed time so I guess I must close.

---

11 Since Charles is nowhere near achieving the five-year residence requirement for the Homestead Act of 1862, even with three years of credit for his military service, it seems safe to conclude that he has decided to get the patent by paying the $1.25 per acre, provision for which is made elsewhere in the legislation. Still, the six months of residence is a sticking point.

Truly your cousin

Frank Johnson

January 16, 1887

Dear Papa,

I wish I could come in the spring tell Jim and bob to hurry and write Joe Emma wanted Joes marble and *says pease buddy.*

Kate Draper

[Drawing of girl with two wagons and two dogs.]

Jan. 17—1887

My Dearest Husband—

Only 4 days have elapsed since I wrote you but I will begin another as I never finish at once you know. Aren't my poor letters getting to be monotonous? How I wish we were together and that would put a stop to letter writing and be much more enjoyable—don't you think so?

Once in a while we have a blizzard up here for a little change. We had the last yesterday which begun about 12 o'clock Saturday night and cleared up yesterday late in the afternoon but the wind did not cease entirely by bed time. Yesterday morning found us completely snowed in—but Joe managed to push the door a little way open and crawl out of an air hole at the top, and after getting spade and hoe rescued the rest of us—who by the way, were very comfortable—in bed, and not the least alarmed. There is nothing like getting used to things. I was awake in the night and knew there was something going on outside from the patter on the window panes.

Mr. & Mrs. Frank Hull spent almost all of Saturday afternoon with us. I like them right well and believe they are pretty good kind of people. She is the only woman I have seen since near the middle of Nov. Mr. Tanner is not at all popular amongst his neighbors, as he tries and does take advantage when ever he can. It is night. Pa & Emma in bed—an unusual thing for the latter at this time as it is not later than 7 o'clock. Jim & Joe are looking over cards & letters, also Kate. Joe reading—which he sometimes does. Arthur and Mame near the stove in low conversation—I mean quiet. I crowed most too early and have to take Emma.

Night of 18. Emma kept me up late last night and then was awake and restless during the night. And I am sure the little thing had the colic. She is asleep now. Jim is the only one at the table with me. All others excepting Pa are around the stove eating biscuits—& tobacco.

I was *so* disappointed to day in not getting a letter from you. Your last was written the 3, and 2 weeks seems a long time to wait and then be disappointed—but the fault is with the mails—or rather in the obstruction of roads. No mail came into Bowdle yesterday. Day after tomorrow Joe will go to office again—for there is no telling what the last blizzard and snow has done. Joe said it was hard work getting to Theodore through the drifts to day. I notice from the card of the new bank that Diffenderfer is cashier. I am afraid you are left out and I should hardly suppose another would be started as you hoped, considering the number of stock holders in the one formed. I am sorry—but don't worry for you can't be without an office long, if you don't get into something sooner. Bless your heart—these people don't know what they are about when they reject you.[12] But it may be for your own good and if we don't see it now, the future may make it plain. Uncle John is ready anytime to get you a situation if you will only say so. But I would prefer to live in Mo. or Ark., wouldn't you? Uncle John has sent Pa several papers. Night of 19. All up but Pa & Joe and it isn't later than 7 o'clock. It has been a very disagreeable day out. It has much the appearance of a blizzard but it may possibly blow over by morning. I do hope so, for I feel as if I can scarcely wait for Joe to go to Theodore and back; I am so anxious to get a letter from you. If he cannot go at all I will hardly know how to contain myself. I don't believe you can know how I long to be with you again. And now if you have no permanent situation you may think best to have us up here still longer. I may feel differently when Spring comes, and I can go out and find recreation of another kind, but now you know it is about the same thing day in and day out. I had better stop for I believe I have run out of material and children are all around the table bothering me any how. Pa has written a long letter to Jim and you must read it for I hope it will be more satisfactory than mine. The children all send much love and many kisses to "good Papa." Love to all dear ones. We haven't seen Mr. J. for a month—or rather he has not been here. Pa & Joe have seen him. Thad comes.

Affy—Yours with oceans of love

Fannie

---

12 Charlie was actually retained as assistant cashier.

Jan. 25, 1887

My Dearest Old Charles:

I can truly say I am once more comparatively happy—for yesterday Joe brought me two such nice letters from you and I don't believe you can imagine what a great relief they were after two weeks of suspense— expecting every other day to get a letter and ending in disappointment. The roads have been blockaded so that mails have not reached Bowdle. Your letters of the 9 and 16 came yesterday. The latter containing a dft. For $25. I still had about $4.00, the rest of the $25 having been spent for coal and provisions for us, by Frank Hull—who made the trip last Saturday in a sled—starting by day light and reached here about 8 o'clock in the night. Pa's and Joe's expenses (if they had gone) would have been at least $2.00 and probably more—and Mr. H. offered to go for $3.00 and we accepted and have been glad as yesterday (their day for going) was cold and a very threatening one. And there we were about out of coal and it would have been necessary to borrow of Mr. Hull for a few days. Now—"all is well with an *abundance* to each & coal. [mark on paper with note: *Emma caused that mark.*] I am afraid Jodie exaggerated things somewhat—but I suppose not intentionally. We are more *pleasantly* situated now and I think it did not extend a week that we did without sugar and then *only* in tea and coffee. *Now* Jim, Kate & I, are the only ones who use sugar *regularly in drinks*—Pa generally takes it but frequently does without. Mame stopped of her own accord because it gives her the headache. Arthur and Joe prefer to make 5 cts per week which I agree to pay whenever able. Yet Joe wanted to do without any how—I suppose simply to show us that he could. I think he has a good deal of firmness of character. It has been about 4 weeks since Mame and Joe begun for pay—and Arthur only commenced a few days since. I use sugar for fruit all the time—and occasionally make cakes, rolls and pies. We have used almost two quarters of beef and 2 hogs since near the 1st of Nov. and some salt meat. We have also had corn, tomatoes, beans and fruit the greater part of the time—and of course other things occasionally—oatmeal and rice. Of course we do not live sumptuously, neither do we starve ourselves by any means.

I'll tell you just what we had for dinner today. Vegetable Soup of Beef—beans, tomatoes and onions—which was pronounced good. I rolled the biscuit dough thin and cut it with a knife and baked to eat with soup. The mean was excellent—and we had good biscuits and gravy and fruit. Now that is a sample but we seldom have soup. That was not a bad dinner by any means. We always have the best of sauces—fine appetites—and therefore all meals are good. Sometimes we have butter too and I mean to have more. Now don't send more money for 2 months at least unless I send for it.

The two dfts. Of $25 each—one in Nov. and the other in Dec. came all right, and I am pretty sure I acknowledged them but my letters are so long on the way and yours also have consumed time, I suppose it puzzles you to keep up with them. I do not think it will be necessary to buy coal or provisions for a month or more at the least. So don't be in a hurry to send more. Don't pay Jodie the $24 for we are about even with Mr. J. We may owe between 4 and 5 dollars but the latter figure well covers the debt and we will settle the rest. If Jodie should ask for it—just tell him that Pa is managing these things up here and is ready any time to make a settlement. You know how accurate he is and can be relied on. As for the mules I hardly know what to say, and I have already written about them several times. I know I felt at times as if they should have been offered for Mr. J's use; but after all Pa may have done what was best, of course he was doing it to your interest, being so afraid the mules would be abused. And I sincerely believe if Pa had not been so considerate for Pete he would have died, *undoubtedly.* You remember what I wrote you about the Bowdle trip when I accompanied Pa? We were in the night getting home and Mr. Terro had to walk from Theodore and pilot us? I would not tell you at the time, knowing how worried you would feel— but it was all owing to Pete's weakness and he would have to stop every few minutes to rest. Sometimes he could only be induced to take about 6 steps before going on and then Mr. Terro would be at the bridle urging him. I know he didn't stop less than 50 times between here and Theodore. I never felt so sorry for any poor thing; and I fully expected him to gradually grow worse and die. But to the contrary (and thanks to Pa's good treatment and is *well and stout.* We will get him [tear in paper] of grain next month and Joe will put the mules in nice condition for selling.13 Joe thinks Mr. Johnson's mule (jack) will not live until Spring— Says he looks terribly and is almost down. They had no mercy on the poor little animals at all even when not compelled by necessity. Joe is also afraid they will lose their bull. Mr. Terro now is giving him some care. Poor Mr. Johnson I do feel sorry for him and even at times felt like offering the mules feeling that they might kill Pete [sic]. Well enough of this for I know you are tired of it. One thing more—Pa—feeling that Pete was not in working order—our own plowing was let alone in order to accommodate Mr. Johnson when he did.

Mame and I have been rejoicing over the good news your letter contained about coming home and long so, for the time to come. *Sometimes* I feel as if I cannot wait and then again I will wonder if you would prefer to have us remain 2 years, and try to make up my mind to

---

13 Such solicitude for dumb beasts was rare on the frontier, it seems safe to say.

that—but I am afraid I would get sick over it. Oh my! What if you should. Well Pa is writing you some kind of a long letter, I presume trying to aid you in some way—he will let me see it, but my letter will probably be done then. *I do so want to see you* you blessed old darling and hope we will not be separated many months longer. But if Carter knows what he is talking about, you cannot prove up without living here 6 months yourself. He ought to be mistaken if he isn't. What does a poor woman amount to? I wonder why a man should ever condescend to marry one. It almost makes my blood curdle when I think of the sacrifices we have made—and now it may avail nothing because I am a woman. There is *nothing just* in such a law. But I yet hope we may get through all right. We will find *Jodie's man* and see what can be done. He was very affable and accommodating. Every body is in bed and I will finish tomorrow.

Wednesday Night, 26

Have you thought of this being Kate's Birthday? Five years old— and she was very much tickled this morning when I gave her her kisses and a package of candy I had stored away—by the way—some you sent by Thad. Well in all probability you have read Pa's letter and may be a little blue over it. I'll tell you what I think. You know different men take different views of the same thing—and all may not look at the law as Carter does. Now we will keep very quiet on the subject of proving up so as not to create any talk up here. You have to talk with Jodie and find out about what questions you will be required to answer and learn the name of the Bangor lawyer he went to before and see what he thinks would be your chance of getting through all right with him—and if he thinks favorable of it—run up when you can as your suggestion was, and leave us to return at your convenience. Or, if he should advise—

send us the name of his Bangor man and we can write him on the subject and see what he says. I know Mr. Kirchoff told me that he had not the least trouble in proving up after his wife had lived on their place 6 months while he was compelled to be away on account of work. Your case is the same, only, we hardly expect to make a home of it. I don't know how he felt on that point then. Now he wants to sell. I feel as if we can get it through. You see from what Carter says—if we have the privilege of proving up—we can *now* advertise at *any time.* You know it has to be done 6 weeks in advance—so we ought to do that before you come, you see.

Write—I know you will though as soon as you can after receiving these letters. We were feeling so happy until Papa threw a wet blanket over every thing. I believe I wouldn't tell Jodie what Carter said—for he will be sure and talk it when he comes back and we might not be able to effect our purpose. Last night while lying awake I thought of other things I wanted to write—and now I am all in a muddle amidst a bustle. Last but not least—I am proud indeed that you managed those men so nicely and went in on your own terms. I know aside from money matters there must be satisfaction in being victorious. I am so glad you will not be so closely confined, and take *much pleasure* in thinking about it. You *blessed old fellow.* I *often* dream of you.

Arthur got a letter from Annie[14] Monday. She wrote about what you did about Mother and Fannie. Others were well. Children are studying pretty well again. I think I shall . . . [Remainder of letter is missing.]

---

14 Charlie's older sister, living in Louisiana, Missouri.

Lebanon, Mo.
Jan. 25 1887

Dear Jim

I wish you all was back here I hoape that you all will come back in the spring Annie has gone to toun now Mary Anne is staying at or house now we have lot of fun at school we pleay gypsey take us and lock us sum of the boys play with the girls I wish that Mamie was here to play with us I guess that I will has to stop now.

Good night

Your cousin Fannie Monroe

Dakota, Walworth County,
Wednesday 26 January 1887, After 12 M.
CC Draper

Dear Friend

On 24th our long suspense was brought to an end by letter that came to P.O. a day or two before. There had been snow obstructions on RR's and we had received no letter for more than a week. Your last to Fannie before then was dated 3d. But yours of 9th and 16 removed the suspense.[15] I received one from Jimmie closed at night of 13th. I hope his strength increased so as to enable him to make a pleasant and profitable Mashfield trip. I suppose he is there now. As Fannie writes to you at this same time, I leave details of newsy matters, if any, to her and con-

---

15 These letters are not in the Draper-McClurg Family Papers.

Carolyn Doyle's small-scale representation of the soddy filled with the Drapers that long winter conjures up the feeling of claustrophobia that must have attended the family.

fine myself to thinking suggestions for your future action, looking at the subject in its various phases, thereby trying to assist you to see where your interests or happiness may lead you. On other subjects I will only remark that Fannie received a draft by last letters and the other two had been received and spent. We were again [illegible] in getting coal, flour, beans, and hauled from Bowdle on very good terms. Mr. Hull was going with sled and he hauled out 1000' coal, 200' flour, 60 beans, some meat, coffee etc. for 50 cts. more only than it would have cost us cash outlay, to have made the trip and we could not have started before 24th, as we had no sled; and the weather was threatening a blizzard. But none came and 25th was a bright, sunny day. So is this day. He got back 7 p.m. Saturday 22d. Our coal would have lasted one more day only. So now we have no fears and presume we can haul with wagon before present supply runs out, say 15th Feby. Yesterday we hauled a load of hay. Small loads only can be hauled in deep snow. The hay we bought from Mr. Johnson & Jodie (12 tons) will run the mules till into April when we expect grass to answer. On settlement for hay deducting cash and mule hire, five dollars or less will pay balance of $24 of hay & qtr. of beef— Now for the suggestions.

According to your expressions, you could "come up here after a while and prove up, make a short visit, go back and Fannie and others go at a favorable time afterwards"; you of course bringing money, $200 and over, rather than mortgage your homestead. That would answer and could be done if no legal obstacle. But you will see from Carter's letter to me here enclosed, that you can prove up only after your own personal residence for six months prior to presenting proof. There fore this plan falls to the ground. Of course you can't come and remain 6 months without giving up your situation and making an entire change. I take it for granted you will not do this. Then comes the question: what can you do to hold your land and acquire a legal title? Should you so decide and not grieve your family to death, you could do this: considering your 3 years army service, you could prove up at end of two (2) years from 18 July last, one year from 18 next July, giving notice in advance and spending last 6 months of that time here, say from 18th July to 18th January 1888. That brings up the reflection of separation from wife and children and you and they for that. [sic] To do this would require your family to remain here two crop seasons; would require either a pair of horses or of mules or two yoke of oxen. In the spring, oxen will cost, good ones, at least $125 a pair, I think. But the re-breaking of which is now broken would cost, each year, not over $30, which might be the best. It would be if you relinquish. As to selling the mules, or if worked in the spring, they should have grain, commencing in February. I do not believe mules and horses will command anything above low prices before a harvest, say for yours $300 or $350.

Then, if that be not agreeable, you could consider the idea of your land now broken being cultivated, gardening done, etc., wheat or oats or both sown, etc. that all may present a good appearance and sell your relinquishment in the fall of this year, after harvest, when, if we have a good harvest there, will be a land boom in Dakota. Of course that is presuming we will have a good crop. Then tree claims also might be relinquished and sold. They might possibly be sold in the spring, but at low prices, I think. I don't look for a boom before a good crop.

So I see nothing else for you to do unless you prefer to abandon your homestead, but to reside here till end of two years (you personally the last six months of same) and get a clear title, or your family still remain till coming fall and sell a relinquishment, having to risk a crop season.

Of course you could at once take family back to old home, if it could be so managed as not to be considered an abandonment of your claim, and no sale be made till a price to suit be offered. Joe and I could come over from our claims and cultivate it and the tree claims also, as it must be after filing. But in any and all such cases, there will have to be either a team or plowing hired. I doubt whether a suitable team can be had from Mr. Johnson.

Now, I may be mistaken about a boom. It may come in the spring but I do not think it will.

Possibly you could sell relinquishment to someone in Laclede who wishes to come here. But your not leaving your family here etc. might be too discouraging for a buyer.

One or two facts worth considering are: a homestead proven up remains one and is not liable for former debts and does not call for $200 to be paid for same. To prove up and convert a homestead, by paying

$200, changes the title and is not longer a homestead and is liable for debts, so that a homestead or sale by relinquishment seems to be the best for you, if no abandonment. To complete homestead or sell in the fall, either requires land now broken to be re-broken and cultivated [illegible] no team.

Of course we are all much gratified to know you have a good position. I presume you can keep the insurance business up to what it has been and probably increase it. I think you will feel much better contented with your family at old home in Lebanon. I think they will not be contented to remain here without you and probably even with you. But Fannie will write of this, of course.

I propose to fight it out on this line and perfect a homestead, if I can. Joe will stick it out, I think, and if we can get properly started we can live and after awhile realize more than a mere living. But just how to get the means for a proper start, I do not now see. But a way will be provided, I believe.

I want you to think on these things and to think fast and let us know how to calculate as definitely as you can. We must soon have seed and all sich.

As to weather. Thermometer is about 0 to 20 below usually at coldest time of day, at intervals lower or higher. Snow that fell first blizzard, 22 November, is still here and occasional falls of 1 or 2 inches more remain also. There has been no melting. There is a depth of 4 to 24 inches according to the surface of the ground and the driven snow sometimes clearing off and at other times filling up. But there is one long and wide unbroken white sheet as far as eyes can see, and this will give water and such moisture is re-assuring good crops.

We are all very well and enclosed is much love, if you can find it. Give love to all.

Truly & afftly
JW McClurg

Morning, 27th, bright, sunshine beautiful, lovely, all well.

Feb. 9, 1887

My Ever Dear Charlie:

My last letter to you was by Thad and now I will get another ready and send when I have an opportunity—which may not be until Saturday and in that case it will not go from Theodore until Monday. Joe may take letters over tomorrow if it is a fair day but we can't expect much mail (and may not get any) before Saturday—and plunging through deep snow and drifts make it hard on rider and horse. Joe frequently is compelled to get off and then he and mule will tug to get a solid footing once more. So you see it is no easy matter to go to P.O. and then we are so often disappointed as the Bowdle mails are very irregular on account of snow obstructions.

Joe went for mail yesterday and brought back a nice lot. I wish you could have seen us. It was better than any 4 of July. I received yours of 30—the only one since yours of 16 and I know one of 23 must be snowed in somewhere. When our mail—*good homeletters*—are hindered you can hardly imagine the disappointment, privation and suspense which come to us. I never before knew so well how to appreciate good letters and we are situated to enjoy them fully—and they brighten our little world more than any one can tell. The $25 draft was enclosed in your letter. I have about $10 besides. Dont send any more until I tell you—you old blessedness.

I wish you could see our surroundings and you would laugh at the idea of my taking a little walk. It is hard work going from here to the stable. In some places the snow is firm sufficiently to bear a mule and in other places you will go down from 1 to 5 feet—so it would be so much on a tugging order there would be more work than recreation. This was a beautiful morning and Joe went after hay but now the wind is blowing snow which will make it very unpleasant for him. Pa has not been helping him since his touch of rheumatism. I will get dinner now. I have the headache and don't feel in a humor for anything. Emma was wakeful last night and of course I did not sleep well.

It is now Thursday morning and I think not very early yet. I am writing by lamplight as we are snowed in with very little day light. I notice a small air hole at the right hand corner of the South window. You see it drifted most terribly last night and snowed and blowed. Another blizzard which commenced yesterday afternoon. Joe has been to the barn and says it is still snowing and blowing—wind from the N.W. Children are getting up now and Joe says it is late. Pa sleeps with his watch under his pillow. It is night. While I was getting breakfast Pa looked at his watch and it was 5 min. to 9. Our house looks as if someone had taken it and chucked it into the snow with the intention of burying it. The high drifts just about cover the front of it—and in going in and out it reminds me of a jack rabbit's hole. We have snow steps and they are made new more frequently than is either necessary or desired. After all I believe it is a necessity as it would be irksome getting out without them. Don't be uneasy about the roof "honey" for the wind keeps that clear of snow.

Mr. Hull has made another trip to Bowdle for us and we have plenty of coal and provisions. I believe enough to carry us to the middle of March any how, and about $30. Now be a little slow about sending more or you will tempt us to be extravagant . I hope you will think best to have me advertise, and at the expiration of 6 weeks (we get ready in the meantime) you come up and prove up and all go back together. Even that would take us into April unless you decide before you receive this. We are having such a terrible winter that we cannot begin to realize that Spring is so near and of course such a thing as a garden seems a long way off—but if Pa returns with us there will be nothing for us to do in that line as Joe will make some arrangement with the Johnson boys.

I am more and more convinced each day that Pa should not be allowed to remain up here—and I hardly think he wants to, but I think looked on it for a while as a matter of course. He is proud spirited and never in the world would have suggested going back with us, yet I really believe he is pleased at the idea, although he says so little. He is very cheerful and loves a practical joke as well as ever. I wish Jim could spare poor old Joe something as he can never need it more than he will in the Spring. Of course he wants to make some improvement on his place and he hasn't a cent to begin with. Sometime he talks as if he will hire to someone for a farm hand. He says he will get along some way and does not intend to go back and does not want to. His model may bring a patent and who knows but that his fortune is near at hand.

I believe Mr. Johnson feels less about selling his farm than ever—and furthermore I know he doesn't want to bring them (his family) here. Why Charlie if there should be another drouth they would only be eating up their substance and bringing nothing in. If he can only hold the farm, that ought to mean their living, and would with proper economy. I say hold on the farm. He thinks he can prove up without them and get the land any how. Poor fellow how I pity him. If ever a man had a troublesome hard winter, he has. I suppose Thad told you the bull had died. Jack (the mule) died a day or two since, and others have died since Thad left. Don't tell any of Em's folks, for if Mr. J. wants them to know he will write them. I have an idea he tries to keep these things from them.

A few minutes ago Joe said there was no prospect of the blizzard giving way. He says he is "awful tired" of digging out of the snow day after day for it is hard work. It seems now as if we could never have anything up here but winter.

Do you think this morning I walked out to the side of our house next the tent between two high drifts—it was blowing so badly in my eyes so I could scarcely look up, and out from the door in front the snow is higher than the doorway so that it was shut from view and I walked on past it, thinking I was going straight to the door. I was perfectly surprised to see how very easy one could be lost any distance from the house. Don't get uneasy now for we never venture to the barn at such times and seldom outside the door.

Look here old fellow don't lie awake and think about your wife and children or any thing else at nights. Just wait till we come home and then I want you to write up our Dakota trip. I will give the points and some ideas and you can do the filling and I know can make a tiptop story—and you see it will have a substantial foundation. I suggested it to Pa one day, but he will never do it. Arthur & Mame may be able some day but they can't now.

If you ever have an opportunity I would like to have you see a simple rhyme that Mame sent the Herndon boys in reply to—"Peaches are good and Apples are better. If you love me write me a letter." signed J.A. Herndon. Dorris's[?] and Archie's initials are the same. The idea occurred to me and I had to write it for her and she copied it and wrote it nicely

A picture shows the roof of a house with a chimney with smoke blowing to the left. On the right side is a partially covered window, and in the front there is a clear window. Otherwise, the place is buried in snow up to the eaves.

too. Don't tell any one for the world. Pa said it was good. I thought it was kind of cute and wanted to get up some fun for them. Their answer doesn't amount to much but they leave her to guess who the right one is. I don't think she cares much about answering, but they might have fun out of it. I think I shall go to bed and finish tomorrow night. Pa has been in bed a long time—Joe, Jim and Joe have just gone. Kate is preparing. Emma is asleep, Arthur & Mame are talking by the stove. I hear Clara's name. They never want to go to bed. We will be snowed in again by morning but we get fresh air from the east window.

Friday night. 11.

You wouldn't begin to know our place if you were dropped down near it in the snow and high drifts so greatly changes the appearance of all surroundings. A little distance from the house towards the stable it looks something like this if I can make you understand. You know I can't draw. The window that shows is the South and belongs to our room that you floored. the part all snow is the addition and [illegible] is an opening in the snow where you go down to the door. And you do not have to step 6 feet to get to the opening as my picture shows. That beautiful r[16] is the only place where that part of the roof is visible. The ravines are wonderfully filled up. And you can scarcely tell where the barn is, as the snow is about on a level with it towards the ravine.

Joe was most of the day digging the way on out of the snow preparatory to hauling hay tomorrow. If we had made a sled the beginning of winter it would have been the thing—but probably now by the time we could get lumber the snow will be leaving us. I am afraid he will have a hard time tomorrow. And he wants to go to P.O if he can also. I am so sorry I couldn't get my letter off before but it could not be done.

Pa and Joe and Emma are in bed. M is writing. A & Jim playing chequers. Joe and Kate drawing. Kate drew those pictures in her letter to you. She never wants any one to give her any help and she is very quick. She is so fond of chequers that she has been neglecting her lessons lately. Joe McC is only one who never plays. Pa is about as fond of it as Kate. Mr. J. moved himself and cattle a day or two ago to Mr. Tanner's—or it was his intention. The blizzard may have prevented. I am so very glad you anticipate more leisure from work, then you can be with us more and I hope have your share of enjoyment and rest. Bless your heart, you deserve it.

It might be very pleasant indeed could you and Mr. Zook[17] start

---

16 Refers to her drawing.

17 John Zook, CC's brother-in-law, Eliza's husband, in Louisiana, Missouri.

a Bank together; but I should like it to be at Lebanon wouldn't you? Has any thing ever been said on the subject by him?

I am glad your desk is more pleasantly situated but don't look too much at the pretty girls. Does your hearing grow better or worse? One night I dreamed it had greatly improved, and the very next I dreamed you were very hard of hearing and also so very sway back with a sore back that you could not straighten your self. I thought Em laughed at you, but that I was miserable and wondered how she could laugh and I awoke. I do think of you so much but then how can I help it? Don't let Mr. Carter's letter bluff or discourage you, but come along and Mr. J. says he knows we will have no trouble. I do so much want to advertise and hurry matters up. I advise you not to spend any money on this place further than proof, for unless we are here, it surely wont pay. People are careless with their stock, giving little heed to the law, and I dont believe it would pay to buy seed. If some one could do something on the shares it might be a good thing. If we only knew just what we were going to do then we could arrange accordingly. Emma is awake and I must take her. Good night dearest and pleasant dreams—love to all. Mr. Johnson I believe intends returning when Joe comes back.

It is Saturday morning, and all is serene. I hope you will be able to read this letter but it seems kind of mixed. I hope you have already decided to have me advertise. I would love to be on a farm too, but not without you were within walking distance. [Scribbled writing] Emma bothers me so. We have suitable [illegible] should we return in April sometime sometime [sic]. I hope I am not worrying you.

I wish you could hear Emma talk. This morning I gave her some biscuit dough and she says "Ankty Mama." She loves to have us talk of you and will say "Papa, candy apply" meaning Apple. You will have to bring an apple in your pocket. She tries to say what the other children do. Kate is a sharper[18] and bad with it.

Mame has finished her History and has taken up grammar. Arthur has gone through his but is having some review before giving it up. He wants to study Philosophy. If you think it worth while for the time will you please see what kind is used there and send him one. Get the most complicated for I am sure he can grasp it. He is anxious for it. He will take up grammar Monday. Jim and Joe are studying some but I am afraid they are not progressing as they should.

I believe I have written enough for once. Joe will try to go to Theodore after hauling hay—and I am almost afraid to look for a letter. But I want one bad. I suppose we may look for 'old Jodie' soon. It is ever a treat to think of the Lebanon news he will bring us.

Give my love to Sallie and Tom—Jim & Mattie [illegible] and Em and love and kisses to each of the little folks. No one can know how dearly I love them all and how much I want to see them. Emma has just put her little arm and hand about my face & says "Seet Mamma."

The children join me in hearts full of love and many kisses to their "good old loving Papa."

Affy
Fannie

Joe's eating his lunch and will then go to P.O. on foot. It is about 25 below 0. He brought hay and says the travelling is awful

---

18 Caustic.

Walworth County, Dakota, 12 Feby, 1887
Saturday. 9 1/4 a.m.
CC Draper

Dear Friend,

I have written Jimmie this date and Fannie as usual writes you. All together you get the details of news, if any, and incidents that have transpired; as to winds, snow, blizzards, etc. We have coal, flour etc. until I think we can haul. If not we can have it done. This morning is nice, beautiful, and moderate for Dakota at this time of year—not many degrees below 0. Joe is preparing to start for hay to do until Monday and in afternoon he expects to go to P.O. These letters then should leave there 14th. All of us here are well and noisy and comfortable. Joe has the coldest work, a part of each day, shovelling away snow, etc.

Fannie has written you no doubt that others (than Carter) think you can prove up without residing here in person 6 mos. preceding. Some of the lawyers may know how and Jodie J may be able to give you the name of one at Bowdle. We will shortly expect a definite letter from you of instructions. I will make no further suggestions until we get such a letter.

Your mules are now so that I have no fear about them. They will be able to work or in condition to be sold in the spring (if a buyer); especially if we soon begin to give them grain. But for all this they must be properly cared for and not overworked. We will treat them right and if not sold will give them all to do that they should do, in plowing.

Much love to all
Truly and affy
J.W. McClurg

Of course Mr. Johnson will write as to their cattle, etc.

Feb. 13, 1887

My Dear Charlie:

Mr. Kirchoff is here and intends going to Bowdle tomorrow and for fear that my letter sent yesterday may be delayed at T. I will send this card any how. Joe got back last night about dark and was so lame from pulling himself through snow sometimes almost waist deep, that he was little able to have gone further had it been necessary. He is still lame to day and about worn out. He will know better than try it again under the same circumstances. He brought me your letter of 23. Tuesday I expect to get yours of 6. This is a lovely day. The little ones play jacks some on Sunday and all generally get a bible verse any how. We have no regular Sunday school lesson. Mame is writing Clara. Pa reads his bible about the whole of Sundays. I haven't much more time on Sundays than other days to spend on leisure reading instead of sewing becomes like Sundays.

Affy

Fannie
Fourteenth of February [1887]

If I could only give worlds of love
How strong my power would be
But none could ever know how much of this
Would always be for thee

There—as true as blossoms grow on
The vine, I am your own true valentine

Now dearest never say I am no Poet after such an effusion. The children are all anticipating Valentines next mail. This has been a bright clear but windy day—blowing snow terribly. Joe wanted to go for hay but there was too much wind. Tuesday 15. It must be after 9 o'clock now and I have first succeeded in getting Emma down and will write a few lines, and depend on tomorrow night for finishing my letter. I am so busy with my housework and patching that I have no time during the day for letter writing. Emma's nap was too long today, and I will know how to manage her tomorrow. All are in bed but Mamie and she has a book. Joe was about all day digging out the wagon and making a start for hay. A little beyond here toward Terro's the mules stuck twice and became discouraged in the deep snow and it was hard work making them pull out. Finally he reached Terro's and borrowed a couple of fuds [?] and returned and will try the trip over tomorrow. I don't know how he will manage if we have any more snow. The Hulls have a sled but generally are using it. Mr. Johnson has a big thing that they cannot use now and I guess we will try to buy it or borrow that and knock it to pieces and make it suit our bed [?] or mules. Of course some way will be provided. It almost scares me to go out and see such great piles of snow around. I am so afraid we might have a sudden thaw and possibly rain at the same time. And in that case it seems to me we would have trouble. But Pa and Joe only smile at my fuss. Joe says there is not the least danger of our being flooded because if necessary he could quickly cut a hole through the lower side of our house and the water would run out rapidly. He will of course make ditches as soon as thawing sets in. This morning wind was from the South and now it is from the N.W. As yet there are no indications of warm weather. I was hopeful for awhile that we could return home before the melting snows found the streams—but I suppose that can hardly be the case now. I wish I was with you to night you blessed old dearest. I wonder if there is another woman who loves her husband as I do? Good night sweet heart. 16. It is a little while since supper and Emma is on the table dancing around and jumping into Mamie's lap. Kate is near by on the couch. Arthur & Joe are playing out, Jim having been with them but is by the stove now warming a little. Joe is attending the mules. Pa is sitting quietly by the stove. He went with Joe for hay to day and returned with a sunburnt face. It is a lovely day—a gentle reminder of Spring notwithstanding the great masses of snow to be seen on all sides. I have just been playing checkers with A. & Jim. Have also gotten Emma down and it must be between 8 & 9 oclock. We had our Supper between 3 & 4. Kate, Pa and Joe are in bed—the latter snoring loudly by the way. Pa will give him a punch now and then during the night and you frequently hear from Joe. He says Pa often gives him a severe punch when he is lying awake for fear he will snore. Joe don't like it, but he can't help himself. Poor fellow says he don't sleep much some nights. I don't know how it is with Pa when he keeps up the punching. It makes fun for the rest of us. The three boys are in low conversation by the stove. Mame reading Joe's Boys, which she must know by heart. She finished a nice letter to "Aunt Annie" to day. I enjoyed your letter of 23 for it was so full of love for us. Joe will go to P.O. tomorrow and ride. I will surely get your letter of 6. Oh your good letters are like "oil on the troubled waters" and I enjoy one till the next one comes. I have almost obliterated some from carrying them in my pockets.

Feby 15, 1887

Register of Land Office
Aberdeen
Dak

Dear Sir:

In Feby 1886 I filed my soldier's declaratory to 160 acres land in Walworth Co Dak.

In July 1886 I with my entire family, wife & 6 children, made settlement on the land, a house previously having been erected.

In August 1886 I made homestead filing at your Office. Since settlement as above my family has not been absent from the place a single day. In the spring of 1886 I had 10 acres of oats sown which proved a failure. I have 11 acres broken, a good house, barn, walled well—improvements worth between 2 & 3 hundred dollars. My family traveled about 900 miles in a wagon to reach the land. I lived a month on it personally, but as it was after crop time, I had to leave to make a living for my family.

In view of these facts (to be substantiated by affidavits in proof) is it absolutely necessary for me to be personally on the land 6 months prior to making proof, or any definite time, before I can commute and prove up and get a title to my land?

In perfecting homestead is time covered by soldier's declaratory deducted from the 5 years?

Please send me blank notice of intention to make final proof and let me know amt fee to send you.

Yours truly
C.C. Draper

[Answer on back of above letter:]

You must make the land your home for six months prior to your making proof, if this is done you may prove up. Of course it will be well for you to make as strong a proof as possible.

Yours
N.H. Harris
Reg. E

The fee for filing will be settled with the [pr?] by you.

Feb. 22—1887

My Dearest Charles:

I must have a little talk with you before I go to bed for I am disappointed and almost ready to cry. Joe went to PO to day, but brought me no letter from you. One from Jim of the 11 came to Pa and I should have gotten yours of 6 any how but it is stopped some where on the way. I never have been so terribly disappointed since you left us for I know he had some mail and when he said there was no letter for me my heart seemed in my throat for I was not prepared for it. I was glad to hear you were well 10 days ago any how, and if Joe can go again Saturday he may possibly bring me three letters from you. Then wont I have a treat though. I know they are on the way for me if you have been well enough to write. Emma, Kate and Joe got valentines from Col. Springs—I think addressed by Ed. They were delighted, but poor Jim cried. I told him I though you had sent him one that he would get and it soothed him. When I says this is for Emma[19] who was right against me, she was very much tickled and says "goody." Did you think of this being Pa's birthday—his 69 anniversary. I did my best and made a "big dinner." Arthur said he wished his Grandpa's birthday could be every day. I told Joe 3 weeks ago to get me a turkey and he partially engaged it but finally forgot all about it. Still we had a good dinner any how. Well I feel better now and as Pa hates to have us sit up late will go to bed as I have abundance of time for writing before Saturday. Mame is washing her feet or is just through. We wash "pretty nigh all over" sometimes. Arthur is reading. Others, all in bed and Joe snoring. A. is almost through his arithmetic. I do wish he was at some good school where he would be kept up to the mark. He will soon have no study but grammar unless he reviews, which hardly means study for him. His Natural History he has read through and I would be willing to bet knows almost every thing in it.

Feb. 23.

This is one of the coldest days we have had in this month—still it is not very cold for Dakota. I have not observed the thermometer. All are now in bed but Mame, Arthur and myself, and the former is undressing. As I have been washing some to day and am pretty tired I shall go soon. The days are short and we do not get up early so I never undertake much at a time, but a small washing tires me very much. I feel tired most all the time but not as weak as I was in Lebanon. I am tired because there is always something for me to do and not because I am sick. Yet I believe I am thinner than when you were here. Don't that seem a long time ago?

---

19 Fannie refers to the valentine Emma received in the mail.

Poor Mame was homesick this evening and says it seems to her that we will never go back. So Jim[20] thinks I have no grit. Ask him to experiment a little in his own family. I am glad he is doing so well. Does Tom like drumming?

Do you know little Emma would rather talk of you than anything else. In the mornings early she will snug up close to me as soon as she is awake and say "tok Mama" and I'll say what must I talk about and she will say Papa, Kate, lappel, candy, Mame—meaning to tell about your coming and bringing apples and candy to all. She is so unselfish and never wants anything alone. She is cute and smart too, and seems to understand everything. She loves to have me tell her anything at all about you and is always interested.

Feb. 24.

It is night again and I am afraid I have nothing to write, our lives all so monotonous in our little world snowed in from everybody. I have been washing again to day and am tired. Tomorrow I mean to take somewhat of a rest. I put Emma down just before commencing this. Pa & Joe are in bed. Arthur and Kate playing checkers. Mame and two boys having fun with their slates. Joe hauled one load of hay to day. He wants to arrange a trip to Bowdle soon if he can get a sled. Don't feel afraid that we will neglect those things necessary for our comfort. We look ahead all the time and are very careful not to have our larder or coal pile too small before replenishing. It is so natural though that you should think of all this and be anxious that we might suffer. So far this winter we have done admirably and been greatly blessed. Mr. Kerchoff brought some potatoes

---

20 James McClurg is Fannie's brother, a dentist in Lebanon, of whose remarkable grit no record exists.

a few days ago which were quite a treat. I think I can buy some from him. I may find a little more to say tomorrow and will now bid you good night with pleasant dreams dearest. Oh how I want to see you! Friday night. Here I am again and will try to write a little more. I have just gotten Emma down and it is 8 o'clock or after. The 3 boys and Mame are at the table—the former talking animals and supposing big things now and then. The latter reading of course. Joe is by the stove chewing his cud—having been away most all day. This morning it was clear and still and between 10 & 11 o'clock he started to Mr. Kerchoff's (to have his hair cut) and by the time he got there a blizzard was in the air and wind from the N.W. it being from S.E. when he left home. It progressed rapidly and blew terribly all the rest of the day, but somewhat abated about 5 o'clock and he go home near 6. Mame and I went to the barn at the beginning and it was hard walking and my nose just ached by the time I reached the house—we were facing it then you see, but it must have grown 6 or 8 times more severe in a short time. You know if there is snow on the ground it blows it with that coming down, and it is an impossibility to face it and see any thing, it is so fine and cutting. I was relieved when Joe came in. It is blowing some yet and cold. If Joe can, he will go to PO tomorrow. Oh I am so anxious to hear from you again through one of your nice letters. And am rather impatient to know what you would like to have us do. Kerchoff wants to sell badly and told Joe to day he would sell his relinquishment for $350 including a wagon, team and plough. He has a first-rate barn and a good house and a small chicken house—26 acres broken. They are burning hay and Joe says he was not comfortable while there. Joe thinks something of going to Bowdle Monday if weather is good. In three more days we will have Spring and it is like the middle of winter. I shall never forget this winter. I suppose Thad and Jodie have left home before this. We are all anxious to see them and particularly Jodie as he will give us the news. Those darkeys made a good escape but I am glad they were not hung. They may learn a trade and be more useful when at liberty again. I presume you are having such beautiful weather that your mind is on gardening, strawberries and such like. Can you be induced to put in some lettuce and onions when it is time? Tell Sallie to sow tomato seeds in a box and I will relieve her of some of the plants when I get back.

I have been trying to rest to day but still feel tired. It may be partly from such close confinement. I have been trying to take Dr. Dayo's medicine but can't remember it regularly and am afraid it will do no good. I thought as spring was approaching I would be more liable, probably, to another attack of Erysipelas. I have had no symptoms that I know of. I will close now unless something prevents Joe from going tomorrow.

I will feel younger and a hundred percent better if I get a letter from you.

Give my love to all dear ones and I do want to see them more than anyone can tell. We did not know how pleasantly situated we were before I left Lebanon and I hope when we get back we will at least try to remain together. Grit! Grit! Grit has nothing to do with it! Oh pshaw! Why cant we all see and feel alike. A few short years and we are gone. You old darling I want to be with you, but if you want me to stay up here I shall willingly submit. With a heart full of love for you, I am your Affectionate Wife, Fannie—

Saturday morning and wind blowing pretty hard. I am terribly afraid Joe will not go to Theodore. He is sitting by the stove waiting further developments I suppose. He has always been very good about going for our mails. The wind blew pretty hard all night. Some of the children are now playing chequers and others looking on—all but Emma around the board, and her Grandpa has her. I have only swept this morning and our dishes are unwashed. Much love for you from all of us and kisses from the children who would love dearly to see you and delight in talking of you. Poor Mame will have spells of despondency in spite of every thing. Love & kisses to Sallie & little ones & Tom.

Affy—Fannie

Feb 26 1887

Dear Papa:

I got your letter to day and I was so glad. You owe Joe a letter too. Mama is writing for me with Emma in her lap and Emma grabs the pencil and trys to write and Mama can harly write sometimes—

I wish you were here to take me riding on a sled too and then I would have some fun. I run out sometimes and get so cold that I cry sometimes when I come in. [Handwriting changes.] I got Marys letter and answered it old prince and pete and alec are fine. I will be glad when spring comes so we can go Home the Boys can walk on there snow shoes. I have 20 pictures pasted on the wall Jim hardly ever plays on his harp now. Emma will try to say any thing you tell her. We are all tanned and Mama says we get blacker ever day. Joes as freckled as a turkey egg.

Good bye
Kate S. Draper

[In Fannie's handwriting]: My bible enclosed Kate's letter. It had only been there a week. Now don't censure me for I try to be a good girl.

THE WINTER IS WANING, *although March hosts more blizzards and below-zero weather, but the family is delighting in opportunities to get outside—even to the point of going barefoot! The children's education still receives much attention, although Fannie is sometimes worried about the progress. Plans for spring planting recur, and disposing of the mules continues to be a preoccupation. The decision about going back to Missouri seems made, but there is still enough uncertainty about it to allow some anxiety on Mame's and Fannie's parts. Fannie continues to do all she can to discourage the rest of the family from moving to Dakota.*

Mar 3, 1887

Dearest—

Only a note. Joe will soon be ready to start. Brought back $7.82 and I have $9.00 and something here altogether something over $16.00. Am all right. Sent a letter by Joe but he mailed it late next morning instead of when just getting there. Consequently it did not go with a lot of mail that was sent off to Ipswich in a wagon that same morning. I was so sorry but it couldn't be helped I suppose. Wind from the north and rather cold. Willy Hill sent the children a sled and they will have splendid coasting for awhile anyhow. Expect two or three letters from you as a goodly pile of mail reached Theodore yesterday or the day before. I can scarcely wait for Joe's return.

Joe is ready.

Affectionately,

Fannie

Piles of love to one and all. Children send love and kisses.

(Other side) Don't bother about seeds. It will be a dead loss *if we return* for Pa *must* go with us. And Joe can do nothing without a team and hiring labor *will not pay us at all.*

Walworth County Dakota, Thursday, 3 March, 1887

Dear Friend,

I write this for Fannie and self. All are very well. We expect Jodie shortly; presume he is snowed up. Mail now carried irregularly by wagon west of Aberdeen. In a week or less time train looked for at Bowdle. On first Joe went to Bowdle and returned yesterday with coal and supplies with Pete and Alie to a sled. Weather has been very favorable for four or more days. The first snow thawed some (first thaw) but it froze again that night and did not thaw yesterday. So Joe was favored with good road for sled. He goes today to Theodore and we expect mail. This kind of weather the snow will go off slowly and go into ground. Mr. Johnson is well also. No general news. People do not travel about. *We want that letter from you.*

Seed etc. will now be needed for farming and gardening. Much love from all to all.

    Truly & affly,

    JW McClurg

March 9—1887

My Dearest Charlie:

    Joe will soon start to P.O. It seems as if I am never going to write you a letter again. Joe is impatient to start now. He made the Bowdle trip yesterday. He brought back nearly a thousand lbs. of coal, and we had a fair supply already. We are all right until May any how, and longer if weather is warm. This is a lovely spring day. Joe brought back Jodie's trunk and that *treasure* of a box which we were too impatient to leave closed over night. I wish you could have seen us. You blessed old darling—just like you to remember us in that good way!

    Joe had just finished his supper and Thad opened this box with myself Pa and every child around looking on but Kate who was too sleepy to stay awake, and went to bed with a promise from me to wake her when the box was opened. We tried our best but did not succeed. The box was opened with many exclamations of delight from each one and *what richness* before us. That butter we tasted for breakfast and as we have been doing without, with the exception of about 2 lbs within the last 4 or 5 months don't you know it was a perfect treat? I cannot tell you how much we enjoyed it and thought our breakfast fit for a queen. We had to have a little cheese too for a change and it was good. We mean to hide some of that delicious fruit for dinner. Oh yes those nice apples were tasted last night (but of course I had to refrain) and this morning our breakfast plates were each decorated with one. The children have been eating candy and nuts since, and I ate one of those nice prunes.

Well, last night I took one of those butter boats and filled with goodies and put a tablet and calendar on top—ready for Kate's birthday present from you, and this morning early Jim was whispering in her ear and she was all excitement and after looking at her box—said this day & Christmas were the best days she ever had. Joe is mad and I must stop.

Love & kisses from your wife and little ones

Affy—Fannie

Mail is at Theodore and I am expecting a treat. Tad left us this morning being here 2 days.

----

lebanon Mo March 17 1887

Dear Jim

I received your welcon [sic] letter some time ago and I was glad to here from you. Well Jim I have not very much to wright about this time. I will will [sic] awful glad when you come back wont you. I have not told JAT aubot [sic] it[?] Arthur told me &[?] forgot it I will tell her the next time I see her if you wont me to. Jim do you like to live out in dakota how big are Jack rabbits. Ed and me are going to leave our traps out there till next winter and then it will save us the trubble of cary them out next winter [illegible] it I would like awful well to have you come back. There is going to be a family come from Chicago and move in Kopp house I hope they have got seven or eight boys don't you about our size we will have fun then wont we well I will close. I will wright to Joe in the morning I half to go to bed now it is ten oclock so I will close.

I remane your old pardner Bird Dodd

March 21, 1887

My Dearest Charlie:

This may be the beginning of a long letter—but if Joe will only go to Theodore today it will be the reverse as he will want to get off as soon as possible. He has been very good about going for the mail but must be allowed to pursue his own course—so even Pa never insists on his going. He has a most unpleasant disposition.

We have just had a two day blizzard. Jodie has been with us as he got back here (from his Papa's trip to Bowdle) the evening before. We had a nice visit with him and this morning he left for Mr. Tanner's and wants to move to his own shanty tomorrow. I suppose Mr. Johnson will get home tonight and there will be great rejoicing in that house. Jody says he went off in fine spirits with his mind fully made up to sell his farm. I want him to do what is best for himself and family but it makes me heartsick to think of their farm home being sold. And I know Em and her girls will never like it up here. It means confinement in the winter and mosquito fighting all the long summer. The flies are also very troublesome and are bad here now. It may be the best thing Mr. J. can do as he has the land here—but knowing it will be so unpleasant for the others why can't he be induced to make some other investment and not come up here—provided he does sell. I wish you would tell Em what I have written. *I know* they will have *many regrets* if they ever come up here and *never* be satisfied. The boys can get along and partially enjoy it but it will be hard and never pleasant for Em and the girls.

I suppose now we can hardly expect to get home for strawberries, but we may be able to inhale their perfume, and everything will seem lovely with you in our midst.

Pa says if you are here after the expiration of six months and make your proof it will not be necessary to wait for return but you can make satisfactory arrangements with some lawyer. I do hope there will be no trouble.

I intend planting a few early seeds—lettuce and radishes and onion sets that we can eat in April and May. It does not look much like seed time now as everything is again white with snow and drifts high in places—but they can soon disappear with the return of warm days. This is a clear day with wind from the west and pretty cold but a big improvement on the blizzard as that surely dropped the mercury 15 or 20 below zero. We cannot realize you are having warm sun shiny days, yet know it is the fact. I hope there will be no cold snap to destroy peaches that must be well advanced. How *can* Mr. J. sell and leave his peach crop behind? Joe will not go to P.O. until tomorrow and still I am afraid I can only give you a short letter for I have so little to write about. The children have all been studying this morning—and Mame and Arthur are still reading and Jim, Joe, and Kate looking over our collection of stones. Mame and I were almost sick last week from colds (which the warm weather brought us) and I let their lessons go altogether. I will be so glad when we get back as it is hard to manage the children all living in a huddle and so closely confined. What children would be angels—but I do not mean that ours are so bad—yet they might be better. Kate is pretty bad, but she is teased considerably.

Mame and I had a walk a few days ago, the first we have had since about the middle of November. We went on the high places where the snow had melted—but the ground of course was not. It is now night and

I will close my letter. I have just put Emma down. Kate is asleep and Pa is in bed and has been for some time. Mame is near me leaning with her arms on the table. The poor child hardly ever feels well but of course she needs outdoor recreation. Jim is at the table drawing. Arthur and Joe are talking trapping, catching turkeys and ganders; little Joe an attentive listener. I have not yet received your letter of 27 but may tomorrow with one of 13 which ought to be here. I have not broken the last $25 sent. Will have to get meat and flour soon. I want to try and economize all I can when we get home and assist you in paying debts. I hope you have gotten yourself a suit of clothes. I may yet have to send for a few more things before our time is up. Even children can do a good deal of damage in two months and we may have to be here longer. Joe has on his best pants now but I will try and rig up his old ones tomorrow. Arthur's that I have already patched two or three times are more holy than righteous now but I shall make one more effort any how before giving them up. Jim is doing very well in one of Arthur's pairs made short. The are not a very snug fit and he wears suspenders with them.

I wish you could have seen Jim just before discarding his felts. They were terribly out of shape and large enough for John Estes. Arthur will give you a sketch when in the humor. He don't feel like it tonight. I have one somewhere (drawing by Jim). If I can find it I will enclose it. When you don't wear rubbers with the things they eventually become all foot.

Aunt Neal wrote that she would send me a photo of Sue and Will and I may get them tomorrow. She writes that Uncle John was looking worse than she ever saw him and that he was thinking of having Dave take his place in Leadville and he go to the ranch and have a rest. They were building a barn and getting along nicely. Still want to get us up there.

Well, old dearest, I will close and let all become dark and quiet for the night. Does it seem as if the days would ever pass and our time of meeting come? And still the time is flying rapidly by. I was sorry to hear of Mrs. Young's death. I know her daughter, Mrs. Stone, will so sadly miss her, for I believe she was a very affectionate daughter. With much love and many kisses from your wife and little ones.

Ever fondly,

Fannie

Love to Sallie, Jim, and Em and their partners and kisses to all little ones.

Theodore Dak. March 29, 1887

My Dear Papa:

I would have written to you before but as Mama writes to you regularly all the time I was afraid I could not tell you anything new.

Mama and I finished washing the supper dishes about an hour ago.

It has been a warm, pleasant day, and the children have been out playing a long time. I went out for awhile, but I haven't run around for so long that I was soon tired out. We played on that old house near the well.

The snow is all melted from around the top of it and it's good and dry.

30.

It is another beautiful day, tho' not quite so nice as it was yesterday, but is melting as much, if not more. Uncle Joe hauled 4 loads of hay yesterday, and one today, and he thinks he can finish hauling all of it today.

Mama and Arthur have just gotten through washing the dishes.

Usually I wash and Arthur wipes them, but I have not been feeling very well for the last few days. Kate is hunting for her book—Word Method. Whenever she gets started at her lessons she don't know when to stop, but gets lesson after lesson until we get tired out hearing her.

I am over to Percentage in Arithmetic and I am "stuck." I can't understand it. But if I get much behind my class I can study in vacation. I am studying physical geography and like it as well as anything I ever studied. I am in Harvey's Practical Grammar and am over to adjectives. I was never in this grammar before, and it's pretty hard, and besides I don't like it a bit.

Jody stayed with us last night. He had been out all day getting in cattle to herd. Kate is studying her lesson and this is the way she spells pretty—"p-r-e-t-t-y".

I want to go home so much. Wont we all have a good time in the cars coming home? We all send heaps of love.

Your loving daughter,

Mame

March 30, 1887

Dear Papa,

Arthur got tired and didn't feel like writing so I thought that I'd write. Mama is making the biscuits now. Arthur found a grass hopper today. The snow is melting some today. Mama is reading out loud to Arthur. We play out doors where the snow is off sometimes. Little old Emma wakes up in the morning and says talk, Mama, talk.

Good bye,

Joe Draper

Dear Friend,

I join in, but have nothing to say of consequence, there being no news of a general or public kind. And, of course, Fannie, Mamie, and others write all about family. We are now near the close of another day (30th) and a fine one: wind from the N.W. but the sun thaws the snow and ice and they are going off just as we like to see—giving up no overflow, but wetting the ground and filling wells, lakes, pools, holes, etc. We have freezes at night and thaws in days—real sugar weather in Missouri. Today Joe hauled three loads hay and yesterday four, the last of the hay purchased from Mr. J. and Jody. It will run the mules until sometime in May.

Most likely Joe will make a Bowdle trip next week for supplies if weather remains good. I think it will hardly be necessary to have more coal now; probably not at all, that depending on the time the family shall leave here. Jodie stayed here last night. He is out to engage cattle for herding the season. He and Thad are well. All yours are well. I am in my usual good health. Sometime since I thought I had a touch of rheumatism for two or three days in one hip but it tapered off and has not returned. We are anxious to learn what now are Mr. Johnson's prospects for selling out this spring, as I presume his bringing the family here depends on settling.

You have no idea how your three boys are growing, especially their legs. They talk of strength and activity—of going at one jump from house to stable and outrunning a RR train—including the girls, they are also progressing.

Truly & affy, love to all

JW McClurg

March 30 1887

Dear Papa,

Mama and Grandpa are playing checkers and Arthur and Mame are reading. Just now little old Emma diped her finger in the ink and rubbed it on her face. Kate can play checkers pretty good. She beat Grandpa she keeps count how many times she beats him she beat him 21 times it is night now and we have been playing pretty Bird in my cup [sic]. Papa I thank you for the caps you sent me. Mama is getting Emma to sleep and Uncle Joe is getting ready for bed. Papa I cant think of anything else to say, so good night.

Jim Draper

[Note from Fanny attached]:

Mame's letter ought to be read first as hers was the first written and there are repetitions. Jim's and Joe's were not written as well as usual as the little fellows were not feeling very much like writing.

Jim and Mame are going to Theodore with Joe. No water of any consequence anywhere.

Arthur wrote his note about bed time last night and did it hurriedly.

Affy—

Fannie

March 30, 1887

DEAR PAPA

CAUGHT PRETTY CARLO. OLE. O. A. WILL. YOU. HENS. LAMBS. MARY. BOYS. FORT. WELL. LIKES. THAN. SHOULD. NICE. THEM. LARGER. ALONE. HOOP. FAST. SICK. ROLL. ONE. GROW. LIE. VERY. YOURLITTLEGIRL. KATE.

---

31 March, 1887, 9:00 a.m.

Beautiful morning—now thawing some—nice and clear—all feel well. Joe will soon fix up wagon and go over to Theodore for the mail of 28th and 30 (if any) and for such supplies as flour, etc. Mamie and possibly some other will accompany him, for benefit of good fresh air. Arthur, Joe and Kate are out romping, Arthur having the advantage of legs. Snow and ice have melted down till it is only in the lower ground and is fast disappearing.

Love & truly & affy,

JW McClurg

March 30, 1887

Dear Papa:

I commenced a letter to you two or three hours ago but I felt so bad that I had to quit. Most of the snow has melted off, and it is warm though there was a tolerably stiff wind from a little N. of W. We boys go barefooted nearly all the time. I guess Uncle Joe will go for the mail tomorrow. He has hauled nearly all of the hay.

I have invented another mode of locomotion for a small boat. Here is a drawing of it. A crank turns the big wheel which is connected with a small one by a leather band.[1] Jodie stayed all night with us last night and went over to Hoven today. Hoven is over in the German settlement. I haven't seen a gopher this spring but Mr. Kerchoff says that the prairie dogs are out. I will try to do as you told me about the philosophy.

Will you please send me a little rubber?[2] I want a very small one for the band in my model.

I saw seven ducks flying north the other day; and a week or so ago I saw a killdeer.

Well, I guess I'll have to stop, so goodbye.

Your affectionate son,

Arthur

Tell Annie I will write to her soon. I keep forgetting it.

Mar. 30th/87

My Dearest Husband:

This is not my day for writing but I cant resist the temptation of sending a few lines with Mame's. The boys want to write too but I am afraid will not settle down to it. Yes Jim will but I am doubtful about the other two, who are now bounding over hill towards Hulls—barefoot.

---

1 There is a drawing of a boat with wheel amid ship and a belt going to a paddle wheel in the stern.

2 Rubber bands that come around envelopes.

Don't be alarmed! I am not careless with them but you know they must be out after their long confinement and the melting snow makes water everywhere. When they wear shoes they come in with wet feet—often soaked and I concluded the bare foot was better for them—then when they find dry places their feet are warm and when they come in are soon comfortable and never get the least cold in doors. Arthur has a pair of felts he draws on when he goes for water as there is snow all the way. The boys seem quite hardy, also Kate and Emma, the latter looking a little delicate. Mamie's health is not first class.

Our question now is what shall we do with the mules? A sale for cash will be hard to effect considering the hard winter and apparent scarcity of money. What do you say to trading for cattle provided we get a good thing and say 75 or $100 included? We may be able to get some such trade out of Baunberg as he wants to leave—but he has said nothing. Or would you be willing to trade for stock alone? We could put them with Jodie's herd until about middle of Oct. We might make a good thing out of it as cattle are low now. Let me know soon what to do. Joe will take charge of things when we leave but he says he would or could get along nicely with the oxen if they were gotten in a trade. I mean a yoke and would use and take care of them. Sometime in June he has agreed to take charge of Jodie's herd, then he would be glad if the mules had been disposed of as he could not give them the attention he would like to and they would probably grow shabby. I will write to send by Monday's mail.

Love and kisses from wife and babies—
Affy—Fannie

April 7—1887

My own Dearest:

Little Emma is standing near me by the South window and we are the only occupants in doors. It is a most lovely day and the children are enjoying a romping play before work begins and I am having a little rest before doing my morning's work. I am tired and weak this morning as you have often seen me at home when in a worthless condition. Tell Sallie she will be disappointed if she anticipates an improvement in my looks. I am so glad her and Tom's health are so good now. Pa received her letter yesterday which of course we all enjoyed. It is good to think of Miss Mary being one of us again. Give her my best love, and I shall be so glad to see her again. Pa is enjoying the warm sunlight this morning and Joe is giving mules attention which he rather delights in. He finished hauling hay with the exception of some about covered by water, which he says will be good to put on the barn after awhile (if it is not stolen). We have been very lucky in not having any hay stolen and Joe thinks we have enough to last through May.

We are feeding mules some grain now and with an abundance of hay they are looking first rate. Pa and Joe are now over hauling things in the tent. We still have a good deal of snow in places and our little ravine is full of snow and water. By evenings the little brook is so musical as can be and I love to stand outside and listen to it. If it would just stay there how nice it would be for this place. Mame and Jim have come in and the former is reading to the other. He is as fond of reading as A. & M. Emma is calling Kate & getting so troublesome that I will have to stop. When I sat down & commenced writing, she says, "wite to Papa, Mama."? I have been lying down awhile and got Emma asleep, who always crawls in by the side of me when allowed. Arthur and Mame did up the dishes—then

I got up and swept, and a little redding up is needed yet to do our little shanty justice. Mame is lying down awhile now. She is feeling some better than for several days. She was disappointed yesterday by not being able to go to Theodore as a slight colic interfered and she was afraid of its becoming more severe. Kate went and she and Jim returned feeling bright and fresh after their ride which both enjoyed very much. Tomorrow Joe may take the wagon again and then Mame will go if well enough & day is suitable. When Jodie was here a few days since he said they would go to housekeeping just as soon as they could move stove & would have been up there now had they known the valley could be crossed, which was then the case. The Tanners had told him it could not be crossed. He said Tad was the greatest boy just to talk any way, and we oughtn't to believe any thing he says. Poor old Tad—he is a right pleasant boy and our children all like him. I do hope some thing may bring about the proper change to make a true man of him. "God's Grace can save unto the uttermost" but I hardly believe that is the exact quotation.

Brunberg does not want to buy mules now as Joe saw him yesterday, but he will look out for others. Your good letter of 20 came last Saturday & tomorrow I hope to get another. Each Saturday is hailed with delight by me—when the sky is clear. Your letter of 27 Feb. has not come yet & I do hate to have to lose it. Jim was tickled with his fine valentine, particularly, as his from Col. Sps. never got here. I am afraid you will be disappointed with the children's advancement when you can examine them, as they have lost considerable time necessarily. This pleasant weather it is almost impossible to confine them. They are all out now at some rocky point. Emma is standing out in the sun near the house. I don't want Mame to study now & that makes it harder some to compel the boys.

You are working too hard old fellow & not sleeping enough, and I want you to put a stop to it. Rejoice with me that March is gone and you may be here in 7 weeks & although I am so very impatient to see you I know those weeks will not be a great while in passing and you will be with us—God helping us.

It is now getting towards evening and Mame and I have had quite a walk which I think I will feel all the better for. The ground is very damp yet, and grass full of water but a few days like this will soon dry up every thing, and there we will go "rock picking" as Kate calls it, and roam around like birds out of cage. Mame and I are already planning a picnic to the gulches when you come if you can take time for it.

Jodie was here this afternoon on his way home with his stove Etc., preparatory to his housekeeping. He was right successful in getting cattle to herd or at least got fair promises, and was in good spirits and reported Tadlock [illegible] two men (in a sleigh) were across the stream today (too deep to cross to this side) talking to Pa and making inquiries about vacant claims, tree claims etc. They were intelligent men. I think in a short time there will be no vacancies in these parts and we can sell at good figures if we should want to. Who knows but we may yet want to make a home of it but I hope not. Joe has been busy all day in cleaning out tent and digging and cutting ice away from lower part of the house and also took some out from the other room which accumulated during the blizzards. Yesterday he took considerable from front part of the house so our every day paths right at the house are getting in nice condition and we can step out without getting feet covered with mud. The little well house being buried in all winter now stands out in relief independent of its surroundings. If it had not been walled & protected the brook would now be running smoothly over it, but it would be no "laughing matter" to any of us.

Night. All are in bed but me, and I hear snoring from some quarter. How I wish you were with us all. It is about 7 months since you were here. I think that is a long separation for two who love as we do, and I hardly think you can ever induce me to leave you behind again for even a shorter period. I am so sorry you get so lonely. Sundays don your best (I hope you have gotten a suit) and go to Sunday school organize a class *of boys* from the street first, and then set a good example by remaining to church which will please Mr. Bickford and half of Sunday will be gone before you know it and the after noon will soon follow. Then by the time I get home you will be so regular an attendant that of course I will have to go to be with you and that will be added to your credit. See the good you might accomplish. And without jesting you would enjoy it. You know they have always been short of good teachers and I have and will always insist that you would make one of the best. I am gratified to know that Annie thought well of the children's letters. I have one of Kate's to her Grandma and want to write when I am feeling better and send it. I never saw a little thing take so fondly to books as she. It will be the happiest moment of her life when she can start to school & she will want to be kept busy too for it is study she likes.

Good night dearest & best. Yours with all love imaginable. Fannie D. I have just soiled my letter over the lamp having no blotter. Tuesday Morning. It is cloudy but Joe will go to P.O. Geese are going N. & we hope to get one. Jim has had E. out in her buggy this morning. Children send love and kisses. Give our much love to Sallie, Tom & little ones— Em's folks and Jim's. We are anxious to know of Mr. Johnson's prospects.

April 8—1887

My Dearest Husband:

As there is a possibility of Joe going to Bowdle tomorrow I will commence my letter any how. He has been helping Kerchoff sow wheat to day and has not yet gotten in so we are not sure that he has decided to go tomorrow. It is about dark and time he was in. They were intending to go Monday but Mr. Hill sent them word to day that they would have to lose no time in getting seed as supply there was about exhausted & it would not be replenished so they may to tomorrow (Joe & Kerchoff). I should like to get your letter of last Sunday before Joe goes as it may change my memorandum of supply and seeds—some of which I must get.

I feel so little like writing to night. Have a slight neuralgia in my eye and a lonesome feeling in my heart. Jodie read a letter from his Papa, here, a day or two since in which he stated that you would hardly take us back before August. I didn't know what to make of it and have been more or less blue ever since and poor Mame feels as if she could hardly stand it. June seemed a long way off and I have exercised all my mental ingenuity to work on Mame's imagination and bring it closer. If you think it best to have us stay until August and I should have an opportunity (a good one) I would be greatly tempted to send Mame to Louisiana [Mo] –to stay with her Grandma until we go home. Poor little darling she is not well, and you don't know what great delight she takes in making plans for home comforts and pleasure. When we are out together she don't want to talk of any thing else scarcely and I am about as bad. Joe has come in and I think will hardly go to Bowdle tomorrow, but will send to Mr. Hill to secure them and then go Monday. It has been a lovely day, equal to May but cloudy this afternoon, and in Mo. we would say it is going to rain. The snow is still on the ground in some places but the stream in the ravine has grown very small and will soon be only a bed again, but it has given us some kind of enjoyment that only a little stream can and we hate to see it go. This afternoon I sat down east of the well on the bank of the stream and indulged in some sweet melancholy thoughts, Little Emma and I. But we were soon discovered by Mame, Kate and the boys and my sweet reveries brought to a close. Do you remember our fishing picnics at Linn Creek with poor Bill? How good she used to be to humor us when she cared very little for it herself. Our well has a good supply of water in it now. Joe, Jim and I went to Rosetta's & Anderson's yesterday & tried to get butter and chickens, but failed.

I thought I would get 10 or 12 and besides furnishing eggs, would be a "diversion," and we could eat occasionally when we get chicken hungry. We may go somewhere tomorrow & try to find some. Tuesday Pa & Joe went to Theodore—Pa's first trip since Fall, and Arthur went duck hunting, but only got two shots, & they were on the wing at a distance & he got none. There are plenty of geese and ducks in the lake but they are so *very* wild. While they were gone Mame & I basked in the sun near the hay & played I spy with Joe and Emma. Jim & Kate playing some where around. I guess I will not finish this until Sunday but good night old dearest. Oh, how I want to be with you.

Affy Fannie. *Love to all.*

Kate sends the little paintings drawn by one of the boys for her to paint and she thinks they are very nice.[3] She is so freckled now, but well and hearty & fat & a bigger tom boy you never saw.

Saturday: I shall mail this, this morning for fear I cannot send on Monday for bad weather as it is so threatening. I will write soon again. Fannie

---

3 Three drawings: a bird on a branch, a squirrel, and a flower.

April 20—1887

My Dearest Charlie:

How I wish you were here this beautiful April day, and little Joe's 8 anniversary of which he is quite proud. I put a dime under his plate at breakfast and he was delighted. The nice box of candy you sent me came the 16 and was a surprise as I never thought of such a thing as you sending me any kind of a present. We enjoyed it though you may be sure, and just coming from your hands made it doubly good. Mame, Arthur and I have done a small washing to day by spelling each other, Arthur being rather the best man I believe. I am right tired now but probably will sleep all the better for it to night—but have been sleeping pretty well any how lately. Pa and Joe are at work on their claims today—this being the third day Joe has put in over there. He is digging in the hill side so as not to have so much house to build. It is on both claims, as Pa may stay there a few nights (if he goes with us)—and be able to return again before the expiration of 6 months and manage to hold his claim. I think he intends to return with us but I can't get him to say so. They will take dinner with Tad to day as Joe promised to yesterday. They will take a lunch generally, and sometimes Arthur will go and help Joe when Pa does not feel like it. Jodie went to Bowdle yesterday intending to return to day. It will be sufficiently dry in a few days (if it does not rain) to plow for oats. And I think tomorrow we may be able to put in lettuce and onions or radishes I mean. I guess I will stop and get dinner as it must be about 3 o'clock. We frequently take a lunch before that time and children always want something at night too. Not one of them is drinking coffee now but Emma who imposes on her Grandpa.

Our dining is over and dishes washed and children all out having a romping play. It is probably 5 o'clock and Pa and Joe are not in yet. Our principal amusement now is pitching quoits. I enjoy it splendidly and pitch pretty well. Pa plays too but I believe Joe has not yet had a game. I always did like any outdoor sport and think this far ahead of cards and checkers. It is a cold cloudy and windy morning—blowing from the East. Our stormy course you remember. Yet Pa and Joe have again gone to their claims and will remain all day if they can. I saw in the Rustic you had bought the Chapel place. I suppose you will want to put up a stone front as there will be plenty of material right at hand. I hope it will prove to be a good investment. What farm did you and Mr. Diffenderfer get, or I want to know if it was the Wedge farm as there is a bet on it. Pa thinks it was but I do not. I do hope you will realize something handsome from it. Mame and I plan living on it for a pastime, but find pleasure in it—but you know how it is. If we are only permitted to be a reunited family I feel as if I can content myself any where. You old dearest I do so long to be with you. I must surely think doz. of times during the day what day of the month it is, and when night comes rejoice that another day is gone. Another day comes and it is the same thing with only a variation of work. I have altered Mame's and Kate's dresses and have them ready for traveling. Every little helps and I cannot accomplish much in one day. It is too cold for children to play out to day and the three little girls are near me in chairs and the boys are on their bunk telling animal stories. I hear Emma say "talk Mame."

Friday 22.

I will add a few more lines and Joe will take it to the office. It is too bad it will lie there two days before going out. Yesterday Pa & Joe were driven in by the rain about 11 o'clock and the showers continued the afternoon and this morning there was a light snow on the ground & wind cold from the north but it is clearing up. It feels considerably like winter. No playing out of doors to day. Did you get your linen coat I sent by Mr. Johnson? What route do you think you will take us home on? But there is plenty of time for decision.

I got a good social letter from Mrs. Dr. Armstrong a few days since and intend answering it when I feel pretty well. If Mr. J. should sell his farm, do all you can to induce him to buy a cheaper farm near Lebanon if he can find one. Em will be *so dissatisfied* up here. Sunday Mrs. Cartright (Mrs. Cookingham's sister, 17 or 18) came down here on horseback for Tanner's mail with several others, but they did not get off. She is nice appearing and quite pretty. The little flowers you sent us were appreciated and we have one kind in bloom here—mighty pretty. I will send one that has been picked several days. There is still some snow in a few places. I feel as if there was something particularly that I wanted to say to you but I can't think what it is. I suppose nothing of importance.

You can't know how impatient I am for June to come. We yet hear of no one who wants the mules and I hear of some that are buying oxen instead—but of course that requires less cash—a sufficient reason I suppose. I am thinking of advertising them, wagon etc., in a Bowdle paper. Joe spoke to Wilson and one or two about them who may find a buyer. They are looking right well now, and as lively as can be and ought to bring a good price. I suspect we will yet have to find Mr. Lattimer and go back to Missouri as we came in order to sell the team and wagon. It wont cost us more than 50 dollars at the least. What do you think about it? Mame and Kate can return with you and I will make girls of Jim and Arthur and get along finely and it will only be a few more weeks and we won't have so many traps to bother with as we know exactly what we will make use of. I commenced as a joke but think now it might really be a good thing. I know Pa would be perfectly willing, and probably like it.

I fully expect a long letter from you this evening. Your last was short and sweet. *Don't work so late*—it will tell on you and is anything but healthy. Just wait till I get home. If you see Alice Buster tell here to keep herself in readiness. Children join me in much love and many kisses to their good Papa. Give my love to other dear ones whom I long to see—also Miss Mary.

Affy

Fannie

Lebanon Mo

Thursday, April 21 /87

Dear Mame

We were very glad to get your nise letter and would have answered it sooner but I always forgot to do it how are you all. I guess little Emma is pretty big now. Frank can walk a little. Mamma has just finished cleaning house and we havent been going to school that is Loll and I Loll has found a little flowers stuck in it but it looks like[4] there a growing this is what it looks like it is not a very good likeness but the best I could make write to me soon and please excuse my bad writing. Good-bye

From Flora F.

---

4 Picture of house surrounded by trees with fence connecting and a rock lined path to the house.

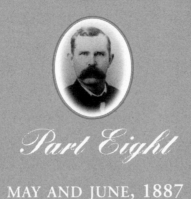

Part Eight

MAY AND JUNE, 1887

THE LETTERS IN THIS CONCLUDING GROUP *are full of the excitement of the arrangements for going home. Fannie is much preoccupied with seeing to it that the family is respectably dressed for the journey. It becomes clear that the Governor is committed to sticking it out in Dakota, resisting urging both from Fannie and Charlie to return with them. Charlie's advice to his father-in-law about the wisdom of getting involved with selling insurance is a classic. These letters also contain a couple of hilarious passages revealing some hazards of breast feeding a child who has learned to talk.*

The last letter is one written by the Governor in the fall of 1888. This letter documents that the Governor and Uncle Joe stayed in Dakota after the rest of the family returned to Missouri. He stayed there until he received an appointment from the Harrison administration to head up the federal land office in Springfield, a patronage job for which the Dakota homesteading experience had uniquely prepared him.

BANK OF BOWDLE

D.W. BURRIGHT   H.G. FULLER

Cashier   Ass't Cashier

Bowdle & Newcomer

Proprietors

Bowdle, Dakota, 5/2, 1887

CC Draper, Esq.

Lebanon, Mo.

Dear Sir:

Replying to your favor of the 26 ult. Will say that we can make you a loan of $300 for 5 years at 11 pr. cent. per annum *without commission* if land is as represented.[1] Hoping that the proposition may meet your approval we are yours truly

H. G. Fuller

May 4, 1887

My Dearest Charlie:

I received another of your good letters on Saturday and will answer a part of it now and enclose in Sallie's. We'll send off my usual letter

---

[1] It seems conclusive from this that Charlie borrowed the money in Dakota to purchase the patent, using the property for collateral.

The one-story house the Drapers lived in before and after going to Dakota was on Harwood Avenue in Lebanon until it was torn down in recent years. They kept the house on Harwood until after the Dakota property was sold in the early 1890s.

Saturday if well enough to write. If you think boy's clothing should be bought in Lebanon instead of Bowdle or Chicago, or some other place let me know and I will send measures, but I think it best to get them on the way. Arthur will need a full suit and shirts (light calico and collar) Jim and Joe only need pants. Pa says corduroy wears splendidly if the quality is good, but if not, it is miserable both to wear and look at. Em might be able to look at it for you and if you think best get it. Hats and shoes we can fit to them in Bowdle and have ample time. Do not get or have made any thing for the little girls. I can manage nicely with what I have and if necessary have Mrs. McClellan sew some. Be sure and let me know what you have done about little Emma's drawers, just so that I can know what to do in the matter, as I don't want her to have two sets. You are mistaken about the wear of our old clothing and very little of it is in shreds. You know washing is harder on clothes than the wearing and ours have not had much of the former. Therefor, we have more than enough clothing (worth wearing) to fill our trunks Pa's included. If you have to pay full fare for Arthur he will be entitled to a box or trunk. You know we have 2 feather beds besides comforts blankets, pillows, sheets, etc. I think by taking one large box that we have here that we can put all in and assign part of its weight to Arthur. I shall write to Mr. Wilson of Bowdle (probably today) and mention articles I have for sale, and he may be able to take them and dispose of them and we can take it out in trade. I have disposed of the wringer. Shall I prevail on Kate to let her little house go? And what shall we do with books?

What do you think of my taking a white girl back with me provided I can get one? The one I am thinking of is under 12 years of age but considerably taller than I, large of age and I have an idea knows pretty well how to wash, iron and milk, if nothing more. I believe I could get for the keeping and a promise to teach her to read and write (as she is a foreigner) and she could soon do all of my work but the washing and I could teach her to sew. And besides it would be a good thing for the girl. Still her parents may not be at all willing to let her go. I will not see them till I hear from you. I am still not feeling well and am able to do so little that time drags. We had a regular blizzard Monday. It commenced sometime during the night and lasted about 24 hours from what we could see and hear. There were snow drifts about 2' or 3 ft deep but the sun soon brought them to tears as it cant be very cold even here in May. A little snow can still be seen in places. I had paid the dollar to Jodie, but was surprised he had written about it. Paid it the first opportunity after my draft was cashed. Jodie is not quite the man he ought to be. Not at all like his good papa nor an uncle of his that I know. This is my business letter.

Love and kisses to your dear self from wife and little ones

Affy

Fannie

Theodore, May 16, 1887

My Dearest Charlie,

I will write a few lines to enclose with Pa's, as I am feeling too tired to write a decent letter and only wrote you a few days ago any how. I wanted to send Arthur's measures and will if I am feeling better this evening. You are probably right in thinking best not to stop for purchases on the way. I should think Tom could get a suit for Arthur in St. Louis cheaper than can be bought in Lebanon. Joe and I will probably make a trip to Bowdle next week and I will buy shoes and stockings and also hats if I can for boys and girls. Mine is still very nice. I will send for Ridley's catalogue to day and may get Mame one inexpensive dress to wear home and myself some kind of linen jack as our worsted dresses will be too warm to travel in. Other things I will manage here so don't worry old fellow. All you have to do now is to attend to Arthur's suit and I will get along finely. Don't get anything for Jim and Joe. You may please send me $25. I had hoped not to call on you for more. This will also provide a pair of shorts for Pa unless Marshall should send him something. He has not written for quite a while. I wish Jim would write oftener to Pa if only short letters for he takes so much comfort from them. Joe is expecting a letter from Jim quite anxiously. Thad and Horace Cartright spent yesterday afternoon with us and were here for dinner. From what Thad said Mr. Cartright wants our mules and may be over in a few days to look at them. I do hope we can sell and at reasonable figures. Can't Tom get Arthur 3 or 4 shirts (calico or percale) in St. Louis? I will send the size of his neck. I hardly think I can get them in Bowdle. It will be rather warm traveling in June won't it? But from [Page missing.]

[Written across the top of first page.] I long for the time. Don't worry any about having home fixed. We will all enjoy that together. Arthur went hunting Saturday and got 3 snipes—one *very* large and *fine*. He killed a duck but couldn't get it. We have had light showers recently but not to amount to much. Rain is needed. Joe is plowing for Mr. Goerr's to day. He will be lost without the mules. Love and kisses from you wife and little ones.

Fannie

May 21 [1887]

My Dear Papa:

I'm only going to add a line and that in a great hurry. We are all well.

It looks very much like rain, but Grandpa is going to Theodore any how and we hope to get a letter from you.

Goodbye,

Mame

Walworth County—Dakota
6½ a.m. Thursday 26 May. 1887
CC Draper

Dear Friend,

Good morning! This is a bright morning. *All well.* Fannie is getting breakfast. "Johnny" is just up and others asleep except Joe McC who is about the mules. I start over to Theodore after breakfast on foot. Joe goes to plowing. Prospects are yet good; but somehow I fear dry weather, but about last of month we may have rain. Fannie has an unfinished letter to you for me to take. She may not write all she would if more time— Therefore I write this and say *particularly:* please do not fail to bring with you, among other things, that *shirt,* open front, *white,* that a mistake was made about. Yours is here and has never been used but the one time.

I hope to receive soon a long letter from Jimmie—I hope his health is better so that he can feel so to do the work that seems to be on the increase. I hope all are well in Lebanon. You see, from this, that economy is a good thing to practice. Love to all.

Truly & affectly

J.W. McClurg

Theodore, May 30—1887

My own Dearest:

Your good long letter Sat. was such a welcome—as your letters always are. Saturdays are always hailed with delight by all of us—particularly on account of a letter from you. Only 3 more Sundays now for you to spend away from us (if all goes well) and wont there be rejoicing in the Draper family. My wringer is the only thing I have disposed of but hope to effect other sales. Mrs. Terro is anxious for the machine and I may get a cow from her. She does not want to pay until Fall but will give the machine and a cow for security and I do not feel like trusting them. I want to see her again and have her give me the cow and if she can redeem her by Fall (1 Oct.) by handing Joe $30 she can, and if unable to do that the cow is mine and Joe can sell her for me. I want to go to Bowdle in a few days and will take carpet and buggy and try to sell them. Some things I can exchange for butter to Mrs. Terro. The $25 draft came Saturday. I am glad you will attend to Emma's little drawers and waists and I will not have them to bother with. Besides Arthur's suit and shirts will you please get him a pr. of suspenders and don't forget my corset. (Dr. Warner's, No. 22) Mrs. Fayant keeps them. You must let us know to the day when you expect to be here, or at Bowdle. The train reaches there about 1 o'clock P.M. and Pa or Joe will meet you and there need be no delay and you can get here by night or before. I hope you will arrange so as not to travel on Sunday. Of course it would add a little to the expense, besides being unpleasant but altogether you would feel well over it I am sure.

This is a real cool windy day and the fire is pleasant. Mosquitoes afraid to show themselves. We manage them now any how. These cool windy days the children prefer to stay around the stove and whittle and listen to Mame read. Jim is as fond of hearing reading as any one and teases considerably for it. They do not say many lessons now. Kate is the only one who really loves her lessons and is always ready when a chance offers.

I have tried to make soap this morning but think it is a failure. A few weeks ago I made some of the nicest lye soap I ever saw and it was beautiful and hard. Mrs. Kerchoff said it was splendid. You know I par-

The Drapers used profits from the sale of the Dakota homestead to purchase this farm on the Tuscumbia Road, north of Lebanon. The Drapers had large orchards and specialized in exporting "fancy" apples.

boil all of the fat meat we use, and that water I set away and skim when it gets cold and keep for soap grease. I saw Jodie a little Saturday. He is plowing on Cartright's tree claim and came down for water. He is looking anxiously for money—poor boy! I almost wish they had never come up here but do hope it will yet prove to be a good thing for them. Joe is at work on his claim to day and will sow flax for himself tomorrow having secured seed from Frank Hull on time. He seems determined to make something out of a little and has more energy that I ever gave him credit for. I wish I could write you a long letter but cant on nothing very well. You ought to have gotten yourself a better suit and I hope can before long. Frank is doing fine with his chickens and ought to realize something from them.

Arthur and Jim are just starting to Terro's for butter and she gives us good sweet milk when ever we ask for it & insists on my doing it. I have been feeling better for a week or so. Am so sorry Em and Jim are not well.

I am thinking you will be surprised at the mature change in Mame. She is leaving her girlish form rather more rapidly than I wish to see—but it is something all mothers have to bear. She is so much company for me.

The children join me in much love & many kisses for yourself. How we all want to see you no tongue can tell.

Affy—Fannie

June 4—1887

My Dearest Charlie—

I made the Bowdle trip all right and got back about sundown yesterday. Mame Jim and Kate enjoyed the trip with us. Couldn't get all I wanted but as Pa is anxious to be off and has been waiting on me I must write again concerning these things.

I now have to trouble you for another draft. 10 dollars will be ample & I am ashamed to have to send for it.

The measure of *Arthur's neck* not allowing for lap is 12 inches. Collar should be 12½ I suppose. It was not the neck band but his bare neck. With *much love* from all.

Affy—Fannie

June 6, 1887

My Dearest Charlie,

I hardly know what kind of letters I have been writing lately. I am afraid not very satisfactory, and as the time approaches for your arrival I feel less like writing and more and more impatient. How I wish the time was here—still it is not very long off and may our good Heavenly Father keep and preserve us that we may soon be a reunited family—oh so happy!

I wrote you hastily that I had made the Bowdle trip. My purchases were all satisfactory but Arthur's shoes—they being one No. too small—and Jodie took them back to day to exchange. I got straw hats for the boys at 50 cts. and very nice too. I did not get Mame a hat as I wanted to—assortment being too small. We will have time at Aberdeen in the evening (as we remain all night) to get her a hat and her old one will answer until then. I think that will be better than your buying in Lebanon for it is so hard to fit without the head. I can surely get what is suitable at Aberdeen and will have nothing else to attend to. Pa can take charge of little folks at Hotel and you M. and I get the hat. Emma loves her "Grandpa". I have sent for Emma a cap and Kate will wear her bonnet. I tried several little ready trimmed dark hats on her and found nothing the least becoming, and her Mother Hubbard looks so cute on her.

The boys have gone to visit Thad to day as happy as larks and will make the trip on foot. I sent him a little butter as I believe they don't buy it. They wore their new hats and Jim and Joe their new shoes and felt considerably dressed up, of course. Kate is out by herself at play—Emma asleep—Mame lazily lounging on the couch near by in our "dining room" and Pa sitting close by, almost asleep—each one trying to keep cool as it is a very warm day.

The days are so *very* long now. This morning I was occupied overhauling boxes and casting aside those things I could dispose of. I am not through yet but had to rest. I took the carpet and buggy to Bowdle but could not find a buyer. Mrs. Peckham would like to have the carpet and machine, but said she could take neither on account of last year's failure—and so it is. Others would like to have them, but there seems to be nothing to spare. I expect to spend the day at Mrs. Tanner's this week and will try to talk them into buying—but I hate to sell them on time.

I may yet be able to sell machine for a cow to Mrs. Terro. The cattle taken a few days ago from them were not under mortgage at all and if he only had money could make the other party suffer. The cattle will be returned to day, and we understand he will be out on bail for the other offense (resisting the sheriff.) Poor Mrs Terro has been terribly troubled over it. Joe is rolling your piece of oats to day. The mules are looking nice now. If we cannot find a buyer Joe is anxious to use them through harvest—making 3 dol. a day and board for himself and team. You can see about it when you come. Of course in that event he will want Jodie to release him from his obligation to him.

Tuesday Morning: Had a little shower this morning but almost clear now & Pa will soon be off to P.O. Emma is begging for titty. I believe if you leave home Sunday night you can reach Bowdle on 1 o'clock train Wednesday. Letters frequently come in that time. We can scarcely wait for the time. Bob is a *pretty bird* with wings partly yellow also neck & head combined with black—not large. They sing very nicely outside and within the past few days he has been singing some. I think he will be a nice pet and would like to take him home with us. If there were no cats I think he could soon be allowed to roam at large. Joe has just gone. No house work done yet. Terro was released yesterday here

Congregational Church, Lebanon, Missouri.

where he came with officer to fix his papers. Pa & I being [rest of sentence missing].

We join one with hearts full of love to their "good old Papa"

Affy—Fannie

Lebanon, Mo. June 8, 1887

Dear Governor:

Your letter was received yesterday making as you see quick time. I shall expect to receive at least a card from Fannie mailed at Bowdle. I am so glad that all of you keep well and doubly glad that you will all so soon be back again in a civilized country. It is only 18 days now until I start for Dakota. Jodie can tell whether I can get there on Tuesday or Wednesday—I have never gone direct by K. City so don't know whether I can make it by Tuesday the 28th but I hope so. Had I not better send for your ticket with ours?

About the Life Ins Agency do not be precipitate,—don't make any engagement till you come home. I am sure you will not like it and the fact of your having so many old friends over the state will only make it the more unpleasant. I know something about the business and it has been done to death—all plans—oldline ordinary life, 10 & 20 yr endowment, 10 & 20 yr annual payments, life & accident, cooperative assessment and all the combinations have had their solicitors over the country till people avoid a life Ins agent like the itch. I was talking with one of them yesterday and gave him my ideas as to the necessary qualifications of a successful agent to all of which he agreed.

He must be *hard headed* and have a brain for scheming and seeing other people's schemes.

He must have eyes that will not see that he is boring the man he is talking to.

He must have ears that will not hear unpleasant things that are said to him.

He must have the cheek of a government mule.

He must have a tongue that will not hesitate to twist and prevaricate to meet the lies of his competition.

He must have feet that will bear an immense amount of standing around and a constitution that will stand the loss of sleep consequent on taking trains at all hours and a stomach that will stand the strain of country hotels.

He must make up his mind to meet rebuffs from old friends and strangers alike. He must be "all things to all men," drink with the boys and pray with the elders, put his feelings in his pocket and a pillow in the seat of his breeches. Now do you think you will fill the bill?[2]

It is singular that you are suffering for want of rain when we have more than enough to spare. All crops here bid fair to be abundant—but Kansas is catching it. Chinch bugs are eating up wheat and oats. You will be here in time to get lots of nice peaches. All well as usual. Jim is still at Waynesville—doing well I have no doubt. If he says anything about a partner discourage it. He does not need one. All he needs is to persevere in what he is doing and he will soon have all the work he can do. When he has more than he can do himself then will be time enough to divide with some one else. I am very glad that Joe is getting in some

---

2 The Governor did not become an insurance salesman.

crops. Truly hope he will be successful. I hope the team can be sold by the time I go up. My love to all.

Affy, C.C. Draper

June 10, 1887

My Own Dearest,

I wish you were with us this pleasant morning, and we would "roam the Prairies over." The atmosphere is so pure and cool and the air so musical with the varied notes of Birds. The cactus is in bloom now and it is beautiful and delicate. As usual I am resting awhile after breakfast—Mame and Arthur washing dishes—boys and Kate rambling. Emma out near by, and Pa sitting close by. Joe went to Jodie's yesterday to assist him with his flax. Intends being back to night. I am sure Joe will have no trouble in finding plenty of work for himself and team at good wages if we cannot sell the mules before leaving and he will give the best attention. You remember Jodie engaged him to herd—taking charge of cattle either in this or next month. A few days ago he told Joe he wanted him to be ready by 1 of July to stack hay for him, and I think wanting the mules also—never once asking if the change would make any difference with him and if he could get the mules. Only talked in his presumptuous way which is disagreeable in any one.

With your permission Joe wants to use the team (if we cannot sell) and I am sure will make money. You can think of it and talk over it when you come. Give Joe the first consideration wont you? If Jodie will treat him right, Joe will be ready to accommodate him knowing of course he can get nothing in return now, and I think will not particu-

This Lebanon public school was attended by all of the Draper children. It was about two blocks from their home in Harwood.

larly care for that any how—but Jodie ought to treat him as if he were *white*.[3]

We are all rejoicing so at the near approach of your coming that it occupies most of our thought and conversation. I am now sure we will have to have two large boxes outside of trunks to hold the things we *must* take home and will *want*. What we cannot sell we must leave in Joe's charge—probably at Jodie's or Kirchoff's. I have not yet seen Mrs.

---

3 A couple of other times, Fannie uses expressions that are racist by today's standard. By nineteenth-century standards the Drapers and McClurgs were notably enlightened in their racial views. Fannie taught slaves to read when it was against the law to do so in Missouri, and her father was not only an advocate of abolition; he also supported black suffrage—and women's suffrage as well. (See Lynn Morrow, "Joseph W. McClurg: Entrepreneur, Politician, Citizen," *Missouri Historical Review,* January 1984, pp. 168–200.)

Tanner about machine. May go to day or tomorrow. See if you can get a redding comb all coarse like the one I had before leaving home. I intended to try to get at Bowdle but neglected it. If you cannot get them let me know and I will send to B. as I prefer that kind.

Won't you please bring Pa a couple of white handkerchiefs? Marshall will not send him any money. About two weeks ago he wound up one his letters by saying "Your money is ready for you." Pa *laughed* and I am sure did not reply to it. I made a few hasty remarks and was rather sorry for it afterwards, but I guess it didn't hurt anything. Joe felt as I did. We will leave Marshall and *his money* to themselves after this. And cheerfully do as we can. Emma is bothering so I must stop awhile. She is 2 years old to day and has given me a kiss or two for her Papa. Sometimes she kisses me of her own accord and says "Kiss for Papa." She is interesting and affectionate we think. Arthur and I went over Mrs. Terro's to day (by the way it is just after supper now (about 5 o'clock) to see her about the machine. She wants it very much but will not know for a while what she can do about buying. You wont buy tickets before leaving will you? It seems to me I would not buy at all for the children for we may be able to get M. & A. through on half price (they are small), and the others free. Mrs. McClellan says on their way here they were not asked a question about Nora & she is near Jim's size. It wont hurt to try any how & if necessary pay on the train. Only 2 more Saturdays besides tomorrow to expect letters from you. You do not know how I am rejoicing all the time at the prospect of so soon seeing and being with you again.

I want to take the children out near the gulches and spend one day before we go back. We would wait for you but know you will not want to take the time.

Pa will go for the mail tomorrow and I may add a line in the morning. With much love to all, and a very big share for yourself and kisses from wife and little ones who are more impatient to see you than you can possibly imagine.

Yours devotedly,

Fannie

June 14, 1887

My Dearest Charlie,

It is after 4 o'clock and also dinner, and as I have just gotten Emma down for a short time will put in a few minutes on a letter to you. The boys and Kate are playing around the old well (their chief resort). It is about Joe's neck in depth and they love to go swimming in it. When they went in first Mame and I each held the end of a rope stretched across it and Arthur took hold of it and walked all around to try the depth. Arthur swims pretty well. Pa and Mame are near me as quiet as church mice. Joe is still weeding his potatoes, expecting to finish to day; and there is a slight prospect for rain just now it may be just in time. We are beginning to need rain pretty badly for wheat and oats and of course another drouth is feared.

Yesterday and to day I went with Pa to Theodore—Kate accompanying us this morning—Yesterday she was sound asleep when we got off, and I think Miss Hubbard had just crawled out of bed when we got there. I went to see her about my machine (but hardly think she will buy). This morning I took my carpet to Mrs. Wright and sold on credit for $4.50 to be paid in the Fall. I enjoy a ride to Theodore early for the air is alive with birds and such a variety of sounds—particularly in Swan lake. The ducks are rearing their young now and add greatly to the noise.

Sunday Arthur scared up a duck with 7 little ones and all the children saw and handled them. But in trying to find them again a short time afterwards they were no where to be seen although they searched far and near. It is raining a little and we do need a soaking rain so badly and we may get it. We had a right nice little shower but nothing like the country needs yet "every little helps." I got your letter yesterday that was written at Mr. Johnson's. It was so good and I love to have you over there for I can think of you as spending a more enjoyable Sunday when you are with Mr. Johnson. I think you will see that Mame has grown considerably too—yet she can wear her gray plaid very nicely which is a little short although I let the hem out—probably three inches or more. Mrs. McClellan has made her a lawn that I brought along. Wednesday about 5 o'clock P.M.—Emma is standing near me with a mud cake spitting on it and rubbing it over her face and hands and begging for "titty." Last night I was partly undressed looking for fleas, and Mame was holding Emma who was delighted at seeing her *favorites* exposed and after laughing and taking on considerably she says "lets suck it." She looks like a little pig now and sunburnt. As much so as little Milburn[4] was last summer. Joe and Arthur went to Mrs. Rosetti's to order butter this morning and were to spend the rest of the day with their Uncle Joe. It has been quite a hot day but windy. I hardly know what to advise you about starting. If you want to get here Tuesday I believe you can by starting Sunday morning. If you leave there Sunday Night I think you will get to Bowdle Wednesday a.m. at 10 oclock. The sooner the better so we can be sure of the time. I have been putting in my spare moments sewing today; and do not feel very tired. Olstein told Pa a few days since that Brunberg had gone to sell his team and some cattle in order to buy our mules. I have

---

4 One of Fannie's brother Jim's sons.

offered machine for $27 but don't believe I can sell.

Must we keep Arthur's saddle. I say yes. I intend sending a box with Pa to be shipped when he goes for you. Will put mirror and one feather bed in. It seems so good to be planning for our home trip. Be sure and have Pa's shirt done up before you come as he hasn't but one white shirt here.

Thursday: Bright & warm after a fine prospect for rain on going to bed. Children asleep excepting Jim who is just about ready for his breakfast. Pa & Joe about off. The former to K's to borrow poney to ride to P.O. I suppose you will have to console yourself with about one more letter from me. Don't it seem almost too good to think of. You don't know how happy I am. I feel better this morning than for a number of weeks & *sewed* yesterday.

Walworth County, Dakota. 2½ P.M. Wednesday 15 June/87
CC Draper

Dear Friend

I write *now* just to be *doing* and to call it the last time, most likely, before you start on your contemplated visit to your Dakota home and for family etc. We now count the days and, in the absence of more definite instructions from you, I expect to start early with mules and wagon, morning of Wednesday 20 for Bowdle, so that we can leave there as soon as desirable in afternoon, the train getting in there now at 10 a.m., when on time. Should you not see wagon or team, by keeping a look out at Elliott & Wallace's (merchants) or at Merchants' Hotel, we will soon meet. Should I be there ahead of you I will be apt to find you at Depot on arrival of train.

Fannie will have a letter to mail, with this, tomorrow, to start 17th. Yesterday I mailed a letter to Jimmie, that went off, of course, this a.m., 15th. He should receive it before starting to Marshfield.

All here are well. Prospects for crops are good, but cannot so remain long without rain. We need it here and may soon get it. Today we are having a strong Southern wind and the Ther. is up to 96 here in the ante-room—storm door room—which we could hardly live without. We are not suffering with heat and I presume plows are running, breaking sod. In most parts of Dakota, judging from statements in papers, there has been plenty of rain.

It is now positively stated that *this season* (fall & winter) a Railroad will be built from Forrest City—on Missouri River S.W. of this to Aberdeen and pass not exceeding 8 miles of this, running by "Hoven" 10 miles of this.[5] *I think this will be & then with good crops,* other roads will come—as to selling mules, money with the people is what is needed. "Brumberg" is *trying* to sell cattle etc. for money to buy them. Jodie and Thad went *south* for some cattle & I suppose got back yesterday—I may add a P.S. before mailing. Much love to all.

Truly & Affectly,
J.W. McClurg

---

5 The Minneapolis and St. Louis Railway actually crossed over what had been the Draper homestead during the first quarter of the twentieth century.

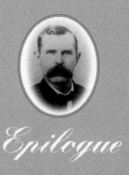

Epilogue

THE CC DRAPER FAMILY RETURNED *to Lebanon, Missouri, the summer of 1887, their wanderlust satisfied.[1] Safe at home, the family settled into the domestic, civic, and cultural life of the town, providing many contributions over several generations. It is interesting—and maybe revealing—that in the many future Draper real estate dealings recorded by the Laclede County Recorder of Deeds, Fannie's name appears often as the main agent in the transactions.*

Charlie spent the rest of his life working in the bank in Lebanon, the first of four generations of Drapers to do so. He continued to sell insurance, and he and Fannie bought the farm on the Tuscumbia Road in the early 1890s and raised and exported "fancy" apples profitably for a good number of years. Later they established a Concord grape vineyard that became a county institution. Charlie was an active Mason and a member of the board of the county horticultural society, and he provided leadership in the Congregational Church. His singing was much enjoyed in a variety of venues.

---

1 Although there is no record of it, it would be only natural for Fannie to congratulate herself quietly on her fine judgment when news of the January 1888 Dakota "Children's Blizzard"—the very next year after their return—reached Lebanon.

This last-known picture of Fannie and Charlie Draper, was taken at their Lebanon farm, where they enjoyed old age together. Courtesy of Western Historical Manuscript Collection (C3069), Columbia, Missouri.

Fannie was active in the church also and was a popular and productive citizen and mother. They died within a couple of years of each other in the early 1930s.

The Governor received a patronage job heading the land office in Springfield, Missouri, in 1889, which brought him back from the Dakota Territory where he had become active in territorial politics and business in Bowdle. The job in Springfield kept him involved for several years, and he died after retirement at the Draper farm in 1900.

Fannie's brother Joe remained in Dakota for a few years, with mentions of his still being there as late as 1894. There are references to his having his own homestead near the one the Drapers wintered on, but details of his arrangements remain to be sorted out. He did return to Lebanon, where he worked on the farm until he died there in 1933.

All the children who went to Dakota led productive lives. Interestingly, except for Arthur, the eldest child, all the children received college degrees, not a common occurrence in rural Missouri in the nineteenth century. Arthur had the opportunity, attending the prestigious Manual Training School (which was part of Washington University in the 1880s) and was thus exposed to higher education, though he did not graduate. Mame, Kate, and Emma all graduated from Knox College in Illinois, Mame and Kate majoring in music, and Emma specializing in domestic science. Both Jim and Joe were educated at the Missouri School of Mines and Metallurgy at Rolla, specializing in civil engineering.

Arthur married Annie Laurie Hilton and became a banker in Lebanon, where he served on the hospital board and school board and was Sunday School Superintendent for the Congregational Church for many years. He was a Mason and served as treasurer in nearly all the organizations he belonged to. Arthur and Laurie had six children who lived, and his family was central to his life, although he was much preoccupied with devising plans for reordering the economic base of the nation—his "ravings," he called them. Arthur was much loved for his humor and his enlightened and generous spirit; the "first rate boy" his mother described became a "first rate man."

Mame married Clint Draper, a second cousin and a theatrical producer specializing in producing minstrel shows. She had a beautiful and well-trained voice but died young as a result of tuberculosis contracted from nursing a dear childhood friend, Clara Wallace, the "Clara" of many letters. She taught music for a time at Drury College in Springfield.

Both Jim and Joe became engineers. Jim had a distinguished academic record at the Missouri School of Mines and Metallurgy at Rolla. Jim married Phoebe Clark and spent most of his career as an engineer with the Kansas highway department, while Joe married Minna Webb and spent considerable time in metallurgical engineering out west and elsewhere. Joe died relatively young and his wife Minna became secretary to Phil Donnelly, a member of Congress and governor of Missouri for two terms. Jim and Joe had one child each.

Kate and Emma both settled in Lebanon, caring for their parents on the family farm and helping with the farm itself. Kate, who never married, taught private music and elocution lessons to several generations of Lebanon's children. She was choir director for the Congregational Church for many years. Emma ran the household and, several years after her sister Mame's death, married her older sister's widower, Clint Draper.

The Johnsons returned to Lebanon within time, also. Marshall had a variety of interests including orchards, a dairy, and other farming activities. Thad and Jodie both wound up in business in Minneapolis after the turn of the century.

It is interesting to note that each of the obituaries summarizing the lives and achievements of Charles Draper, J. W. McClurg, and Marshall Johnson omit reference to the Dakota venture.

RED FRONT STORE

G.C. AURAND

L.E. AMERPOHL

AURAND & AMERPOHL

DEALERS IN

STAPLES AND FANCY DRY GOODS/ READY-MADE CLOTHING

Groceries and Provisions,

Boots, Shoes, Hats, Caps, Gloves, Mittens

bowdle, dakota--------18 _____ 2

. . . sent[?] are a photo of the Republican Glee Club, which I was very glad to acquire. All of the old boys look very natural and it recalled friendship and old times that had almost been forgotten. Is there any prospect of Frank Garett getting married. No doubt friends and acquaintances were surprised to hear of Thad's marriage. In fact I was myself. I knew nothing of it until election day and I had hopes of deferring it until we were in better circumstances financially, or I should have written home at once. We do not intend to keep any thing from you. But if we do it's an over sight. Thad no doubt has a nice-good wife and help-mate.

---

2 The first page of letter missing, thus it is undated. It must, however, have been written in the fall of 1888, more than a year after Fannie and the children returned to Lebanon, because McClurg refers to the election of President Harrison, which occurred in 1888. The Dakota constitutional convention to which he refers also requires an 1888 date. This means that McClurg, along with his son Joe, stayed on in Dakota, Joe until about 1894. President Harrison provided a patronage job for Governor McClurg in the fall of 1889, which brought him back to Missouri. McClurg headed the Land Office in Springfield, a job for which his Dakota homesteading experience had equipped him well.

I am told she has the house fixed up as neat as a pin. Uncle Joe was up yesterday with a load of flax, got $1.20 per bu. If he would follow Thad's footsteps and lead some fair lady up to the matrimonial alter, I think life would be entirely different to him, the poor fellow certainly lives a hard life. I was there in the hills all alone. You remember we are his nearest neighbors and we are a mile away. But he seems to be content. He is another Robinson Crusoe. Has his dog and cat for company. Stemp[?] Cruse (the man we had the words with over the hay last winter a year ago—Bredele[sic] Paterson) is the man we suspect started the fire that burned us out.[3] I haven't taken any steps yet toward prosecution as I haven't had time to thoroughly investigate the matter. But as soon as winter sets in and trade slackens up I will take the time to gather all the evidence bearing on the case that I can and if my attorneys think I have a good case, I will prosecute criminally first, and if I succeed in having him bound over, I will go for him civilly. But if I do not I will drop the matter. Don't you think that will be the best way, as it will make no expense for us. We had a great time here after election.[4] Had a jubilee, firing of anvils, etc. just as if we had been entitled to vote for Harrison. I won $25.00 and a silk plug hat on Gen. Harrison's election. I look a great deal like Harrison when I get on my silk plug hat. I don't make a practice of betting. But I am a died in wool Republican and when ever the Democrats come around making their bluffs, I make them put up or shut up, if I have the money. I was elected as one of the delegates to the legislative convention which meet at Gettysburg. I expect Neel has turned Republican by this time, has he not? Our entertainment at the church the other night went off very nicely. Yes I am sleeping in the store.

---

3 Presumably, this incident occurred on one of the Johnson homesteads in Dakota in the fall of 1887.

4 For a short summary of other McClurg-Draper political background, see Appendix B.

But I don't think that was the cause of my sickness. It's owing to the excessive warm weather for this season of the year. One after noon I took a very severe cold on my lungs which I think was the root of my trouble. Bad colds are very numerous this fall. I haven't the cough I had while in Missouri nor haven't had since here. I think I will continue to sleep in the store until I have built up a trade of my own, —which I think I am doing—So that I know that I am a valuable man for the house, then I can be pretty independent. They have spoken to me about working for them next year. But we have made no . . . [no closing or signature]

Appendix A

This summary is in the Draper-McClurg Family papers in file #97 with materials generated during the 1920s, just a few years before Charlie's death, and nearly forty years after the family returned to Missouri. This was filed with a sketchy fragment of a draft of an article about the Dakota trip attempted, probably, by Kate at the urging of her parents. It seems likely that Charlie summarized this information for Kate's use in writing the essay that she never finished.

Dakota Lands

SW ¼ Sec 8 T. 121 R75. Walworth Co.

Filed Soldier's Declaratory through J.S. Carter, Aberdeen, on Feby 25. 1886

Filed my homestead entry on Aug 30. 1886. Duplicate No 6225. At Aberdeen Land Office.

Went into my sod house on the place on July 29th or 30th. And in the next week or so fixed up house, put in floor, made new room and dug and walled well. Finished well on Aug. 23. 1886

About 12 acres of land broke on the quarter—also good sod stable.

Made final proof at Bangor July 1. 1887
Witnesses. J.M. Johnson
Frank Hull
Before H.C. Grupe Clerk
Sept. 1. 88. Commissioners accepted my proof & reversed Land Office

Land Office informed Carter Oct. 11 1888

Oct 30, 88 wrote the court for permission to make commutation affidavit before cir. Clerk here.

Nov. 13. 88. Sent Carter $200 to pay for land.

Nov. 22 1888
Final duplicate No 9280 issued by order of the Commissioner without affidavits. Apl. 12. 89
Final duplicate sent to Recorder of Walworth Co.

Patent received, #9280. Recorded Vol. 6, Page 46 7 (Recorders Office Genl Land Office) dated Feby 24, 1890. Recorded Apl. 16.89 Vol. 1 page 498.

Sold to F.A. Maines Oct. 3. 92

THE DRAPER AND MCCLURG FAMILIES had been quite prominent in the political and economic life of Missouri in the years leading up to and immediately following the Civil War and were strongly identified with the Republican party. Both families were established in Missouri before statehood in 1821.

The Drapers were prominent in the northeastern portion of the state, prospering in lumber, pork packing, land speculation, and mercantile operations. Members of that family provided leadership in establishing the first rail roads in the state and in keeping Missouri in the Union. Two of them, Zachariah and Philander Draper, served in the state legislature during the 1850s. One family member, Daniel M. Draper, after prominent service in the Ninth Missouri State Militia Cavalry during the war, was elected state auditor for two terms after the war. Charles served with the Third MSM Cavalry, and his father, Philander, was an officer in an infantry regiment before becoming provost marshall in his congressional district.

Before the war J.W. McClurg led a family partnership that operated the largest Missouri mercantile operation outside St. Louis, doing

Congressman Joseph W. McClurg as he would have looked when he was in office in the mid-1860s.

a reputed half-million dollars in trade annually from the headquarters on the Osage river at Linn Creek. When the war began, he took command of a regiment of cavalry in the Missouri State Militia. He also was involved in all the conventions deliberating the course Missouri should follow at the beginning of the Civil War. He was elected congressman from southwest Missouri for three terms beginning in 1862. In 1868 he was elected to a two-year term as a Republican governor of the state.

McClurg's failure of re-election in 1870 was a sign of the return of Democrats to power in Missouri. A coalition of Democrats and the Frank Blair faction of the Republican party combined to defeat McClurg and effect the recapture by the conservative forces of political ascendancy in Missouri. McClurg and his two new sons-in-law, Marshall Johnson and Charles Draper (who had been his secretary during his governorship), returned to McClurg's home base of Linn Creek, Missouri, to revive the economic prosperity that had lagged during and immediately following the war.

Daniel Draper, Charlie's older brother who had been State Auditor for two terms after the war, became so discouraged by prospects in the state (largely because of his identification with the wrong political party) that he emigrated to Colorado, where he spent the rest of his life as a railroad executive. Charlie's other brothers, Edwin and Arthur, also spent most of the rest of their lives in the West, although all three were brought back to Missouri to be buried.

Upon his discharge from the army, Charlie became the personal secretary for the first Missouri Republican governor, Thomas Fletcher. McClurg succeeded Fletcher, and retained Charles as his secretary. He was in that role when he met Fannie, and they were married just after the Governor left office and returned to his business activities at Linn Creek in Camden County, Missouri. He took his sons-in-law, Charles and Marshall Johnson, into the business as partners.

Although the McClurg-Draper-Johnson partnership ambitiously developed new mining and shipping enterprises, the old prosperity did not return to anything like the level enjoyed before the war. After a debilitating lawsuit from a former partner who sued McClurg for using corporate funds to organize and equip a home guard unit to protect the business from bushwhackers at the beginning of the war, the partners liquidated their Camden County assets and started over in Lebanon toward the end of the decade of the 1870s.

The business and political climate became increasingly uncongenial to people identified with the Draper-McClurg political positions, and those considerations may have gone into the decision to go west, where being Republican was no particular liability.[1]

---

1 See Lynn Morrow's "Joseph W. McClurg: Entrepreneur, Politician, Citizen," *Missouri Historical Review,* January 1984, p. 168ff. and Arthur G. Draper, ed. "Philander Draper: Farming on the Missouri Frontier," *Missouri Historical Review,* October 1992, p. 18ff.

Sources

Beard, Lois, *History of Laclede County,* 1979.

Brooks, Allyson, Steph Jacon. *Homesteading and Agricultural Development Context,* South Dakota State Historical Preservation Center, 1994.

Dick, Everett, *The Sod House Frontier,* Lincoln. Neb., 1954.

Draper, Arthur G., ed., "Philander Draper: Farming on the Missouri Frontier," *Missouri Historical Review,* October 1992.

Draper-McClurg Family Papers, C3069, Western Historical Manuscript Collection, Columbia, Mo.

Gleason, Frances, *The First One Hundred Years, A History of Lebanon, Mo.,* 1949.

Hine, Robert V., and John Mack Faragher, *The American West: A New Interpretive History,* Yale University Press, New Haven & London, 2000.

History of Laclede, Camden, et al Counties, The Goodspeed Publishing Co., 1889.

Laskin, David, *The Children's Blizzard,* Harper Collins, New York, 2004.

Morris, Edmund, *The Rise of Theodore Roosevelt,* Random House, 2001.

Morrow, Lynn, "Joseph W. McClurg: Entrepreneur, Politician, Citizen," *Missouri Historical Review,* January 1984, pp. 168–200.

National Snow and Ice Data Center, http://nsidc.org/snow/faq.html.

O'Gara, W.H., *In All Its Fury,* published by The January 12, 1888 Blizzard Club, 1947.

Pictorial History of Laclede County, Lebanon Daily Record, Lebanon, Mo., 2000.

South Dakota Historical Collections, Vol. XIV, "Ranching and Stock Raising in Dakota," pp. 457–58.

South Dakota Historical Collections, Vol. XI, "An Autobiography of a Cowman," p. 512.

Welsh, Roger, *Sod Walls,* Purcells, Inc., Broken Bow, Neb., 1968.

WOMEN
of the
WILD WEST

the lady rode
Bucking horses

PIONEER
Doctor
The Story of a Woman's Work

by Mari Graña

She Wore a
Yellow Ribbon
WOMEN SOLDIERS AND PATRIOTS
of the WESTERN FRONTIER

JoAnn Chartier
and Chris Enss

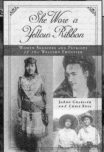

WILD BUNCH
Women

MICHAEL RUTTER

with GREAT
HOPE

Women of the California Gold Rush

JoAnn Chartier
Chris Enss

From entertainer to soldier, doctor to rancher, read about the lives of the exceptional women who pioneered the American West.

- Biographies
- Diaries and letters
- Memoirs
- Regional history
- Westward travel narratives

TWODOT®

TwoDot® is an imprint of The Globe Pequot Press

For a complete listing of all our titles, please visit our Web site at www.GlobePequot.com.

Available wherever books are sold.
Orders can also be placed on the Web at www.GlobePequot.com, by phone from 8:00 A.M. to 5:00 P.M. at 1-800-243-0495, or by fax at 1-800-820-2329.